The Web of Knowledge

Linguistics

Volumes published in this Brill Research Perspectives title are listed at *brill.com/rplis*

The Web of Knowledge

Evidentiality at the Cross-Roads

By

Alexandra Y. Aikhenvald

BRILL

LEIDEN | BOSTON

Library of Congress Control Number: 2021909044

Typeface for the Latin, Greek, and Cyrillic scripts: "Brill". See and download: brill.com/brill-typeface.

ISSN 2667-0682
ISBN 978-90-04-46641-8 (paperback)
ISBN 978-90-04-46642-5 (e-book)

Copyright 2021 by Alexandra Y. Aikhenvald. Published by Koninklijke Brill NV, Leiden, The Netherlands.
Koninklijke Brill NV incorporates the imprints Brill, Brill Nijhoff, Brill Hotei, Brill Schöningh, Brill Fink, Brill mentis, Vandenhoeck & Ruprecht, Böhlau Verlag and V&R Unipress.
Koninklijke Brill NV reserves the right to protect this publication against unauthorized use. Requests for re-use and/or translations must be addressed to Koninklijke Brill NV via brill.com or copyright.com.

This book is printed on acid-free paper and produced in a sustainable manner.

Contents

Preface   VII
Acknowledgements   IX
Abbreviations   X
List of Tables and Illustrations   XV
Abstract   1
Keywords   1
Introduction   2
1 Knowledge through Grammar: A Preamble   2
　1.1 *Evidentiality: Grammatical Expression of Information Source*   4
　1.2 *Egophoricity: Grammatical Expression of Access to Knowledge*   14
　1.3 *Mirativity: Grammatical Expectations of Knowledge*   16
　1.4 *Epistemic Modality: Grammatical Expression of Attitude to Knowledge*   18
2 Links between the Four Groups of Grammatical Categories Related to Knowledge   21
　2.1 *Evidentiality → Egophoricity*   22
　2.2 *Evidentiality → Epistemic Modality*   23
　2.3 *Evidentiality → Mirativity*   28
　2.4 *Egophoricity → Evidentiality*   35
　2.5 *Egophoricity → Epistemic Modality*   36
　2.6 *Egophoricity → Mirativity*   36
　2.7 *Epistemic Modality → Evidentiality*   37
　2.8 *Epistemic Modality → Egophoricity*   38
3 How Evidentials Are Special   39
　3.1 *The Scope of Evidentials*   40
　3.2 *Double Marking of Information Source*   49
　3.3 *Independent Time Reference of Evidentials*   53
　3.4 *Ability to Be Negated Independently from the Predicate*   55
　3.5 *Ability to Be Questioned Separately from the Predicate*   56
　3.6 *Correlations with Speech Genres and Social Environment*   59
　3.7 *How Evidentials Are Special: Interim Conclusions*   62
4 Access to Information and Information Source: Evidentiality Meets Egophoricity   63
　4.1 *'General Knowledge': A Term in an Evidentiality System*   63
　4.2 *Access to Information Source and Knowledge Sharing in Evidentials*   68
　4.3 *Shared Knowledge and Shared Information Source: What Everyone Knows*   74

5 Unequal Relations between Evidentiality and Epistemic Modality 81
6 Dependencies between Evidentiality and Other Grammatical Categories 84
   6.1 *Dependencies between Evidentiality, and Clausal and Sentential Categories* 85
   6.2 *Diachronic Links between Evidentiality and Other Categories* 99
   6.3 *Non-propositional Evidentials: Their Interactions with Other Grammatical Categories* 103
   6.4 *Evidentials and Other Grammatical Categories: A Summary* 108
7 What Can We Conclude? 110
   Appendix: Knowledge through Grammar: Further Categories, Further Options 111
   Commentary 112
   Books by Alexandra Y. Aikhenvald 128
   Index 130

Preface

Expressing knowledge through grammar is crucial for understanding how language works and what it is good for. Evidentiality – the linguistic marking of information source – has been the focus of linguistic investigations for quite a while now. Expressing how one knows things – especially in those languages with grammatical evidentiality where one is forced to do so – has distinct bearings on human communication, cognition, categorization of types of knowledge, and societal conventions. Evidentiality lies at the heart of articulating and communicating knowledge. It is a feature of many languages. But perhaps the most fascinating insights come from those languages which have large obligatory evidential systems – including Tariana and its neighbours from north-west Amazonia. Some 'linguists' with limited knowledge of the languages of the world and a penchant to work just with translations into some familiar European languages – have obscured the notion and the category of evidentiality. Some have confused it with modality – probability and possibility, others diluted it with other concepts – including 'truth', 'evidence', and the like. Evidentiality is not about any of those. It stands apart from other categories, and at the same time interrelates with them.

Throughout my work on evidentiality (started in 2003, as shown in the Commentary to this essay), I have been demonstrating its special status in its many guises. Over the years, there have been numerous studies of evidentials, and their correlations with other means of expressing knowledge. The most valuable ones come from the discovery of new systems and the insights into the immense potential a human language has. This essay comes as a logical step in the progression of our understanding of the phenomena involved and documented to date. Its major focus is on the ways in which evidentials are special, and how they correlate with other categories within language, be it synchronically or through language history.

On 22 May 2019, Junwei Bai, then a senior PhD scholar at the Language and Culture Research Centre, gave a talk entitled 'Egophoricity in Munya?'. The presentation was about the differences between egophoric marking, evidentiality, mirativity and other categories in a previously undescribed Tibeto-Burman language, the topic of Junwei Bai's PhD (since then successfully approved and awarded a rare summa-cum-laude appreciation). During this talk, it all came together for me – the division of labour between various knowledge-related categories and their interactions (summarised in Diagram 1 in this essay, p. 19). This was the foundation for a shorter version of this essay, originally prepared for a workshop 'Evidentiality and modality: at the cross-roads of grammar and lexicon', scheduled to take place at the Université de Montpellier-3 Paul Valéry in June 2020, and then cancelled, as so many events were in that parlous year.

The focus of this essay is the ways in which many grammars of minority languages deal with how one knows things, setting forth a consistent exposure of issues, based on individual grammars and my own fieldwork, and tested through many years of investigation.

Acknowledgements

R. M. W. Dixon provided inspiring comments and feedback on every aspect of this essay. Special thanks go to my colleagues who offered examples, comments and answers to my numerous questions – including Junwei Bai (Abe), Pier Marco Bertinetto, Luca Ciucci, Victor Friedman, Christoph Holz, Gwen Hyslop, Petar Kehayov, Tania Kuteva, Eric Mélac, Anne Storch, Pema Wangdi, and Steve Watters. I owe a debt of gratitude to Eric Mélac for inspiring me to write a shorter version of this essay for a workshop 'Evidentiality and modality: at the cross-roads of grammar and lexicon', originally scheduled to take place at the Université de Montpellier-3 Paul Valéry in June 2020, and then cancelled due to the onset of the pandemic. Janice Wegner supported me in every possible way throughout the writing of this essay, protecting me and linguistics at then Language and Culture Research Centre from disruptive administrative forces. None of this work was done under the auspices of James Cook University. Special thanks go to my teachers of the Tariana language, who keep sharing the beauty of their evidentials with me, notwithstanding the geographical distance between us. And a warm thank-you to Brigitta Flick, for careful checking and proof-reading!

Abbreviations

1	first person
2	second person
3	third person
A	transitive subject and function
ABIL.REAL	abilitative realis
ABL	ablative
ABS	absolutive
ABSTR	abstract
ACC	accusative
ADD	additive
ADDR	addressee
AFF	affix
AFFECT	affected
AG	agentive
ALL	allative
ANIM	animate
APPL	applicative
APPREH	apprehensive
ART	article
ASSERT	assertive
ASSUM	assumed evidential
ASSUM.IMPERF	assumed imperfective
AUG	augmentative
AUX	auxiliary
AV	actor voice
BEN	benefactive
CAUS	causative
CL	classifier
CMPL	complementizer
COM	comitative
COMPAR	comparative
COMPL	completive
COMPL.CL	complement clause
CONJ	conjunctive
CONTR	contrast
CONVB	converb
CONVB.IMPERV	imperfective converb

ABBREVIATIONS

COP	copula
COP.NPAST	copula nonpast
COUNTEREXP	counterexpectation
DECL	declarative
DEF	definite
DEM	demonstrative
DEM.ANIM	animate demonstrative
DEM.INAN	inanimate demonstrative
DET	determiner
DIM	diminutive
DIR	directive
DIR.EV	direct evidential
DIR.INDIV	direct evidential of individual knowledge
DIR.MUTUAL	direct evidential of mutual knowledge
DIRN	directional
DISJ	disjunctive
du	dual
EGO	egophoric
EGO:SAP	egophoric: speech act participants
EMPH	emphatic
ERG	ergative
EST	stative
EV.M	evidential masculine form
EVID	evidential
EVID:GEN.KNOW	evidential general knowledge
EVID:JOINT:VIS	evidential (joint vision)
EXC	exclusive
EXIST	existential
F, f	feminine
FAR.PAST.NONEYEWITNESS.MASC	far past eyewitness masculine
FEM	feminine derivational marker
FNS	final nominal suffix
FOC	focus
FAR.PAST.EYEWITNESS.FEM	far past eyewitness feminine
FUT	future
GEN	genitive
GEN.KNOW	general knowledge

IMM.PAST. EYEWITNESS	immediate past eyewitness
IMM.PAST. NONEYEWITNESS	immediate past non-eyewitness
IMP	imperative
IMPF	imperfective
INC	incompletive
INCH	inchoative
incl	inclusive
INDV	individual
INFIN	infinitive
INFR	inferred
INS	instrumental
INT	intentional
INTENS	intensifier
INTER	interrogative
IRR	irrealis
LIM	limitative
LK	linker
LOC	locative
m	masculine
MASC, masc	masculine
MC	Mandarin Chinese
MIR	mirative
NARR	narrative
NEG	negation
NF, nf	nonfeminine
NOM	nominative case
NOM.PAST	nominal past
NOM.VIS	nominal visual evidential
NOMIN	nominalizer
NOM.CD	nominalizer: classifier/directional
NONVIS	nonvisual
NONFIRSTH	non-firsthand
NSG, nsg	nonsingular
NP	noun phrase
O	transitive object
OBJ	object case, object
OBL	oblique
p	person

PART	participle
PARTIC.FUT	future participle
PARTIC.HAB	habitual participle
PARTIT	partitive
PAST.PARTIC	past participle
PAST.RES.NONWIT	past resultative nonwitnessed
PERF	perfective
PERI	peripheral
PL, pl	plural
PN	personal name
PO	primary object
POSS	possessive
POSTP	postposition
POT	potential
PRES	present
PRES.NONVIS	present nonvisual
PRES.REP	present reported
PRES.VIS	present visual
PRET	preterite
PTV	patient voice
PURP	purposive
PV	perfective
RC	relative clause
REAL	realis
REC.P	recent past
REC.P.ASSUM	recent past assumed
REC.P.NONVIS	recent past nonvisual
REC.P.VIS	recent past visual
RECIP	reciprocal
REFL	reflexive
REL	relative marker
REL.M	relative masculine form
REM.P	remote past
REM.P.ASSUM	remote past assumed
REM.P.VIS	remote past visual
REP	reported
REP.KI	reported, known information
REP.UI	reported, unknown information
S	intransitive subject and function
SAP	speech act participants

SBJ	subjunctive
SEQ	sequential
SG, sg	singular
sgnf	singular nonfeminine
SOC	sociative
SPECL	speculative
SS	same subject
SUB	subordinator
SUBJ	subject
TEL	telic
THEM	thematic
TOP	topic
TOP.NON.A/S	topical nonsubject
TR	transitive
UNWIT	unwitnessed
VCL	verbal classifier
VERT	vertical
VIS	visual

Tables and Illustrations

Tables

1 The grouping of semantic parameters in evidentiality systems   14
2 Links between the four groups of grammatical categories related to knowledge   21
3 How evidentials are special   39
4 The Mamaindê tense/evidential system   66
5 The Southern Nambikwara dual-paradigm evidential system   67
6 'Individual' versus 'mutual' knowledge in South Conchucos Quechua evidentials   72
7 Evidentials and tense in declarative clauses in Tariana   76
8 Non-propositional evidentials and case markers in Tsou   105
9 Nominal evidentials and tense markers in Southern Nambikwara   108

Diagram

1 Evidentiality and other categories related to knowledge   19

Schemes

1 Hierarchy of preferred evidentials in Tariana: a general tendency   11
2 Recurrent meanings in evidential systems   12
3 Mirative extensions of an evidential: a potential pathway   33
4 Mirative extensions of an evidential: an alternative pathway   34
5 Mirative extensions of an evidential: deferred realization: a further alternative path   34
6 Evidentiality and its dependencies with other grammatical systems   99

The Web of Knowledge
Evidentiality at the Cross-Roads

Alexandra Y. Aikhenvald
Centre for Indigenous Health Equity Research, Central Queensland University, Cairns, Queensland, Australia
a.y.aikhenvald@live.com, nyamamayratakw@gmail.com

Abstract

Within the grammar of the world's languages, knowledge can be expressed in various ways. We focus on the grammatical expression of four major groups of meanings related to knowledge: I. Evidentiality: grammatical expression of information source; II. Egophoricity: grammatical expression of access to knowledge; III. Mirativity: grammatical expression of expectation of knowledge; and IV. Epistemic modality: grammatical expression of attitude to knowledge. The four groups of categories interact. Some develop overtones of the others. For instance, some evidential terms may take on egophoric, mirative, or epistemic meanings. Evidentials stand apart from other means of expressing knowledge in their scope, possibility of double marking, time reference different from that of the predicate, the option of being negated or questioned separately from the predicate of the clause, and specific correlations with speech genres and social environment. Evidentials can be semantically complex. They may combine reference to the information sources of the speaker and of the addressee, and access to information source. Evidentials and epistemic modalities display an unequal relationship. Evidentials often arise form reinterpretation of epistemic markers; developments in the opposite direction are restricted. In a situation of language obsolescence, the erstwhile evidentials may undergo reinterpretation as modals, as the obsolescent language succumbs to a dominant one with no evidentials. Evidentials show a number of dependencies with other grammatical categories, including polarity, tense, aspect, person, and number. A few of these dependencies can be explained by the history of the development of evidential distinctions in the language.

Keywords

knowledge – grammar – evidentiality – information source – mirativity – egophoricity – access to knowledge – dependency between grammatical systems – diachronic development – general knowledge – scope

Introduction

How to talk about what you know? And how do you know it, in the first place? Every language has a way of saying how one knows what one is talking about. Cross-linguistically, we find a multiplicity of means expressing information source and pathways of obtaining it. And how one can access knowledge, react to it, and evaluate what one has learnt. The lexical wealth of phrasing inferences, assumptions, probabilities and possibilities in each language can be overwhelming. My aim here is to focus on the relationship between those categories whose core meaning relates to different facets of knowledge.

Evidentiality – grammaticalised marking of information source – is the centrepiece of the expression of knowledge, and is set apart from other knowledge-related categories in a number of ways. Throughout this essay, we show how it is special, when compared with three further groups of knowledge-related groups of categories:
– egophoricity, or grammaticalised access to knowledge;
– mirativity, or grammaticalised expectation of knowledge; and
– epistemic modality, or grammaticalised expression of attitude to knowledge.
I start with a preamble – an outline of four groups of grammatical means related to knowledge. The next four sections address their interface across languages, with special focus on evidentiality. Within each language, grammatical categories interact with each other. A choice in one category may depend on a choice in another: for instance, fewer options for gender, number or tense may be available under negation. In section 6, we then turn to the interactions and dependencies between evidentials and other grammatical categories, both verbal and nominal. The last section contains a brief summary and opens up further questions and avenues of investigation. Additional means of expressing knowledge through grammar are discussed in the Appendix to this essay.

1 Knowledge through Grammar: A Preamble

Meaning in language is essentially coded through two independent but interlocking parts – grammar and lexicon. Grammar involves sets of systems with limited choices – tenses, aspects, cases, genders, and so on. A closed grammatical system imposes limited options on the speaker. If a language has two grammatical genders – say, feminine and masculine – all entities have to be categorised as one or the other. This is quite unlike the lexicon where the choices are potentially open: any language will have a large set of words referring to males, females and perhaps other natural and social genders and subcategories (see Aikhenvald 2015a, 2016: 3–5, Dixon 2010a: 47–54, 2016: 77, Aikhenvald, Dixon and Jarkey 2021, for further discussion).

As Dixon (2021: 77) puts it, 'the basis of language is words and grammar. Speakers work with a range of structural patterns, and techniques for inserting lexical words into them. In this way they can expound an unlimited array of thoughts, observations, feelings, instructions, wishes, hopes, and so on. Meanings are communicated through the medium of sounds for a spoken language, or manual and facial configurations for a signed language'.[1]

In Boas' (1938: 132–3) words, grammar 'determines those aspects of each experience that *must* be expressed ... To give an example: while for us definiteness, number, and time are obligatory aspects, we find in another language location near the speaker or somewhere else, source of information – whether seen, heard, or inferred – as obligatory aspects'. And, consequently, 'the form of our grammar compels us to select a few traits of the thought we wish to express and suppresses many other aspects which the speaker has in mind' (Boas 1942: 182).[2]

In every language, there is a plethora of lexical means for expressing knowledge in its varied guises. These will include open classes of verbs, adverbs, adjectives, nouns, and also parentheticals, restricted sets of modal verbs and particles. Plus various kinds of speech report constructions – an almost universal way of talking about the information one learnt from someone else, in addition to gestures and intonation (more on this in Aikhenvald 2018a: 4, and an example in Vanrell et al. 2014). All these means interact with what has to be expressed within the straightjacket of the grammatical frame. From a historical perspective, a major point of the interaction between lexicon and grammar lies in the historical reality of the processes, and the mechanisms of grammaticalization. This is broadly defined as 'the development from lexical to grammatical forms', covering the ways in which 'grammatical forms and constructions arise and develop through space and time' (the discussion and the definition of the concept is in Kuteva et al. 2019: 3; further discussion is in

---

[1] The discussion in this essay is largely based on spoken languages, for the simple reason of lack of availability of comprehensive studies of relevant phenomena of the expression of knowledge in signed languages (see a brief survey in Wilcox and Shaffer 2018). We hope that future studies will fill this gap. A further component of language is phonology, which has a tangential role in relation to our current investigation.

[2] This is reminiscent of Slobin's reformulation of a similar principle as 'thinking for speaking', whereby 'even within a single language grammar provides a set of options for schematizing experience for the purposes of verbal expression. Any utterance is multiply determined by what I have seen or experienced, my communicative purpose in telling you about it, and the distinctions that are embodied in my grammar' (Slobin 1996: 75).

Heine and Narrog 2021; Aikhenvald 2021a specifically focuses on evidentiality). Within this essay, we will allude to lexical ways of expressing knowledge inasmuch as this is relevant for the grammatical expression of knowledge, and potential origins and development of categories under discussion.

⋯

Four major groups of meanings acquire grammatical expression across the world's languages.

1.1   *Evidentiality: Grammatical Expression of Information Source*

Evidentiality serves to specify the information source of an utterance – whether the speaker saw the event happen, didn't see it but heard it or smelt it or perceived it through supernatural means, or made an inference about it based on visual traces or reasoning, or was told about it. Evidentiality does not have any direct connection with truth or reliability of what one knows – it marks how one knows what one is talking about (see Aikhenvald 2004, 2018a, and the Commentary at the end of this essay).

Having to always mark information source in one's language is looked upon by many – including the general public and journalists – as a particularly enviable feature. Speakers of languages without evidentials wish they had been compelled to always be specific about how they know what they are talking about. As Franz Boas (1942: 182) put it, 'we could read our newspapers with much greater satisfaction if our language would compel them to say whether their reports are based on self-experience, inference, or hearsay!'. This has partly to do with a popular – and unsubstantiated – belief that having evidentials in your language compels you to always tell the truth. In actual fact, the connection between having to mark information source and being truthful is not borne out by the facts (more on this in Aikhenvald 2018a). The main function of evidentials is to express the source of knowledge. One can easily tell a lie manipulating evidentials – all one has to be is smart enough. There are two options – to deliberately use the wrong evidential, and thus tell a lie about how one knows things, or the source of information (for instance, a nonvisual evidential could be used talking about something I had actually seen). Or to use the correct evidential, and the wrong facts – for instance, using a visual evidential to describe what you did not see (more examples are in Aikhenvald 2004: 98–9, 136, and König 2013). One can equally well make a wrong inference, or an incorrect assumption. Truth has little to do with evidentiality. Evidentiality is about being precise. Just like having obligatory tense in one's language does not make one punctual, having to specify one's information source does not make one truthful.

The term 'evidential' in itself is something of a misnomer. It would suggest that an evidential marks 'evidence' for what one says (as one would have 'evidence' in court). An evidential marker in a language does not offer any evidence, or proof: it simply states how the speaker knows something. And no-one will query the information source, nor ask you for any real evidence why you had used it, unless they feel something is amiss. If the audience doubts the speaker's information source, the speaker can add justification as 'evidence' for what they are saying — for instance, adding a lexical explanation 'I saw it' or 'I heard it'.

Having a common word with a different meaning when used as a technical term is not a rarity in itself. Foreign imports into a language are referred to 'loans', 'loanwords', or 'borrowings', as technical terms. From a common-sense perspective, this is a misnomer. A linguistic 'borrowing' or 'loan' is quite unlike borrowing something from someone, or taking a loan from a bank. Once 'borrowed', a word, a morpheme, or a construction will never be given back, and no-one ever pays interest on a loanword. Counter-intuitive as they may be, these technical terms have stuck.

It is not uncommon for a linguistic term to have a counterpart in the real world. The idea of 'time' in the real world translates into 'tense' when expressed in grammar. 'Time' is what our watch shows and what may 'fly' so rapidly. 'Tense' is a grammaticalised set of forms we have to use in a particular language. Not every time distinction acquires grammatical expression in the language: the possibilities for time are unlimited, and for tense they are rather limited. Some languages do not have tense as a grammatical category (see, for instance, Dixon 2012: 9, and Bertinetto 2013). Time words — such as 'today' or 'yesterday' — can also help show what the time is. Similarly, an 'imperative' is a category in the language, while a command is a parameter in the real world. Every language has a way of phrasing commands; but special imperative paradigms are not ubiquitous. Along similar lines, information source can be expressed in every language. But not every language has grammatical evidentials.[3]

---

[3] Further discussion of evidentiality as a grammatical category, its meanings and developments is in Aikhenvald (2004, 2012, 2014, 2015b, 2018a,b). Evidentials and other means of expression of information source are contrasted in Aikhenvald (2014). An up-to-date bibliography on evidentials in every part of the world is in Aikhenvald (2015c); see also papers in Aikhenvald and Dixon (2003), Johanson and Utas (2000) and some in Chafe and Nichols (1986). Earlier approaches to evidentiality which are strongly recommended include Boas (1938), Jakobson (1971); and especially Jacobsen (1986). On the opposite side of the coin, a warning should be issued that Willett (1988) and De Haan (2013) are limited in their coverage and the accuracy of examples, and their generalisations should be treated with caution. The range of meaning which can be linked to evidentiality have given rise to what is known as 'broad' definition of evidentiality in Chafe (1986) which covers speaker's attitude and

The cultural motivation for using evidentials is a requirement to be precise. This resonates with Nuckolls' (2018: 206) discussion of Pastaza Quichua, a Quechuan language from Ecuador:

> Speakers of Pastaza Quichua are careful to clarify the sources of their statements, *not* because they wish to be empirically accountable to objective facts that are verified by means of evidence. Rather, they exercise such care because there is a cultural preference for contextualizing statements within what Nuckolls and Swanson have termed a 'concrete perspective'. A concrete perspective is one which involves specifying the details that make any statement intelligible, such as speakers' personal experiences and memories of specific places, activities, and knowledge about people in their social networks, (Nuckolls 2010, Nuckolls and Swanson 2014).

Information source can be manifested in a variety of ways. Evidentiality is only one of them. Other means – conditional modality, perfect, perfective, or different kinds of complement clauses – may be co-opted to express similar meanings, as what is known as 'evidentiality strategies'. One of the oft-quoted examples is the French conditional – known as *conditionnel de l'information incertaine* – used to express non-firsthand information whose validity is doubtful (see Dendale 1993, Aikhenvald 2004: 106–7, and Alcázar 2018, on other Romance languages). Over time, the meaning of information source, originally just a semantic extension of a given form, may develop into its main meaning. For instance, a perfect or a resultative with an overtone of 'inference' or 'non-firsthand information' becomes a marker of non-witnessed information (a non-witnessed evidential). That is, an evidential strategy will develop into an evidentiality system (see also Friedman 2018). A lexical verb of speech combined with a complementiser is gradually developing into a marker of reported evidentiality, *diz que* or *dizque*, in numerous varieties of South American Spanish, and also in Brazilian Portuguese (see Alcázar 2018). Grammaticalisation is a gradual process; incomplete grammaticalisation of lexical items expressing information source allows us to talk about 'incipient' evidentials.[4]

---

reliability. This all-embracing definition confuses evidentiality proper with related, but different, notions and categories, creating an obstacle for its investigation as a distinct category and obfuscating its cross-linguistic status.

4 See, for instance, Travis (2006) for a systematic application of established criteria for grammaticalisation to the reported *dizque* in Colombian Spanish.

Further means of expressing information source may include lexical means, including verbs of perception ('see', 'hear', 'smell') and cognition ('know', 'understand', and so on). Modal verbs, particles, parentheticals of various sorts, and even facial expressions, can express inference, assumption, and attitude to information – whether the event is considered probable, possible or downright unlikely. Intonation in Pastaza Quichua marks epistemic modality and attitudes to what one knows (but not how one knows things: Nuckolls 2018).

In every language, there is a way of reporting what someone has said. Direct quotations and indirect speech reports may interrelate with attitude to the information quoted or cited. For example, a verbatim quote in Arizona Tewa implies that the speaker does not vouch for the information quoted (Kroskrity 1993: 146). To sound neutral a speaker would prefer an indirect speech report.[5] Similar overtones of 'doubt and lack of reliability' for direct quotations have been described for Karawari, a Papuan language (Telban 2014: 268). Along similar lines, the quotative evidential *tip* in Bashkir – the outcome of a recent transparent grammaticalization from a converb of the verb 'say' – displays epistemic meanings of uncertainty (Greed 2018b: 29–30). In contrast, the quotative evidential in Tojolab'al (a Mayan language from Mexico) does not have overtones of uncertainty, while the reported evidential does (Furbee 2006: 198–9).

The means employed depend on mode (or 'modality') of communication. Storch (2018), referring to Nico Nassenstein's work, comments on how users of social media in rural East Africa 'incorporate screen shots of maps into their text messages in order to present particular propositions as having been eye-witnessed'. The ways of expressing information source appear to be open-ended. Evidentiality differs: it is a closed grammatical system, with a restricted set of options.

Those who speak languages with evidentials complain that the absence of grammatical evidentiality leaves a 'gap'. Victor Friedman, a fluent speaker of Macedonian, mentioned that he himself had felt the absence of evidentiality in his native English after having spent several months in Macedonia (Friedman 2003: 210). Martha Hardman and her colleagues had to 'adjust' their English and always specify how they know things, so as not to upset their Jaqi (Aymara)-speaking friends, for whom specifying information source using evidentials is a 'must' (Hardman 1986: 133). Speakers of the indigenous languages of the Vaupés linguistic area in Brazil and Colombia complain that White people whose languages leave the information source vague are 'liars': they never tell you how they know things. Speakers are

---

5 See Aikhenvald (2004: 139); Aikhenvald (2011: 322) for typological features of speech reports.

prepared to comment on evidentials and explain why they employ them (see Aikhenvald 2004: 339–43, 2020). Evidentials are sensitive to social and technological changes. The choice of evidentials often reflects (a) principles of interaction and attitudes to information, (b) beliefs, spirits, and dreams, (c) speakers' expectations of knowledge, and (c) access to information, oftentimes depending on the kinship relationship between speaker and addressee and speaker's status. As a consequence of their correlation with principles of interaction, representation of knowledge, beliefs and practices, evidentials easily spread from one language to the next in the situation of language contact. They are a familiar feature in a few well-established linguistic areas, including the Balkans and the Vaupés River Basin (more on this in Friedman 2018, and Aikhenvald 2018b).

Evidentiality systems vary in terms of the number of terms and the meanings expressed.[6] Nhêengatú or Língua Geral, a Tupí-Guaraní lingua franca of north-west Amazonia, is a straightforward example of a simple distinction between a reported evidential and an evidentially-unmarked statement (Floyd 2005). Suppose you saw Aldevan go fishing. After that, Aldevan's aunt Marcilha arrives at the house and asks where he has gone. You then reply, *u-sú u-piniatika* (3sg-go 3sg-fish) 'He went fishing'. Then a friend comes to visit and asks Marcilha where Aldevan has gone. She replies, using a reported evidential *paá* – she did not see the man go and knows about him going through a speech report (evidential markers are highlighted in italics).

(1) u-sú   u-piniatika   *paá*   Nheêngatú
     3sg-go   3sg-fish   REP
     'He went fishing (they say/I was told)'

The neighbouring unrelated Baniwa of Içana, an Arawak language, also has just the reported evidential. No other evidential value is expressed (Ramirez 2001: 188–90; author's own fieldwork). The evidential *-pida* is used to indicate

---

6   Translating evidentials into European languages, including English, and glossing them may create confusion. One may have to recur to rendering evidentials with epistemic markers, such as 'apparently' and 'obviously'. Translation of a reported evidential may have to involve a biclausal construction, such as 'I am told that', 'they say that' and so on. These translations do not imply that a reported or a quotative evidential – oftentimes a bound morpheme – has to involve a biclausal construction. Professional scholars need to keep in mind that such translations and glosses are nothing but an approximation, and that one should not postulate any distinctions in the language under consideration based on how it is translated. One needs to beware of those 'scholars' who base their investigations on English (or other) translations rather than the facts of the languages themselves (further details are in Aikhenvald 2004: 7, see also note 3 above).

that the information was obtained through a speech report without indicating its source. It can then be translated as 'they say', 'it is said', or 'I am told'. It can also be used as a quotative. The ambiguity of the reported evidential in the language is reflected in the two meanings of (2) – (a) 'he is eating it is said' and 'he is eating-he says (quoting him)'. The evidential marker is polysemous.

(2) li-iiñha-ka-iina-*pida*   *Baniwa of Içana*
    3sgnf-eat-DECL-INCEPTIVE-REP
    (a) 'He is eating they say' – reported meaning
    (b) 'He is eating he says' – quotative meaning

Jarawara, an Arawá language from southern Amazonia in Brazil, has a two-term evidential system. The language distinguished firsthand and a non-firsthand information source whose expression is fused with past tense. A typical conversation in Jarawara is as follows. One speaker asks the other (Dixon 2003: 168):

(3) jomee   tiwa   na-tafi-*no*   *Jarawara*
     dog(masc)   2sgO   CAUS-wake-IMM.PAST.NONEYEWITNESS.MASC
     awa?
     seem.MASC
     'Does it appear that the dog woke you up?'

He uses the non-firsthand evidential in his question: he didn't himself see or hear the dog; perhaps he was just told about this. The other speaker – who had indeed been woken by the dog and thus saw it or heard it or both – answers using the firsthand evidential fused with immediate past:

(4) owa   na-tafi-*are*-ka   *Jarawara*
     1sgO   CAUS-wake-IMM.PAST.EYEWITNESS.MASC-DECL.MASC
     'It did waken me (I saw it or heard it)'

Evidentials in Jarawara are distinguished in the past tense only, and the expression of evidentiality is FUSED with tense. Indeed, in many languages evidentials are restricted to past tense only: this is intuitively plausible, as the source of information is easier to gather for what has already occurred. We return to this, and other dependencies between evidentials and other clausal categories, in section 6.

Within a single sentence, one clause can be cast in non-firsthand, and another in firsthand evidentiality. In (5), 'Wero had been asleep. He must have descended from his hammock (the narrator infers that this happened, although he did not see it), and then went out of the house (which the narrator did observe)' Dixon 2003: 169).

(5) Wero kisa-me-*no*
 Wero get.down-back-IMM.PAST.NONEYEWITNESS.MASC
 ka-me-*hiri*-ka
 be.in.motion-back-REM.PAST.EYEWITNESS.MASC-DECL.MASC
 'Wero got down from his hammock (which the speaker did not see), and went out (which the speaker did see)'

The non-firsthand, or non-eyewitness, evidential, is polysemous. It refers to the information which had not been acquired by vision or hearing and which may have been inferred. Similarly, the firsthand evidential spans a number of information sources: it may refer what one has learnt through seeing, hearing, or smell.

A larger system of evidentials may offer a more fine-grained set of grammaticalised information sources. Tariana, an Arawak language from Northwest Amazonia, has a system of five evidentials partly fused with tenses. Tariana is closely related to Baniwa of Içana. In contrast to Baniwa of Içana, Tariana is part of the Vaupés River Basin Linguistic Area, which partly accounts for grammatical differences between the two languages.

Evidentials as exponents of information source in Tariana have the following meanings.
– *Visual evidentials* are used if the speaker has seen the event or the state, or the event can be easily observed.
– *Nonvisual evidentials* refer to something heard, or smelt, or felt by touch (or something one cannot quite discern).
– *Inferred evidentials* refer to something inferred based on visible results: for instance, that it has rained because one can see the puddles, or that someone has eaten chicken because their hands are greasy.
– *Assumed evidentials* are used if a statement is based on reasonable assumption and general knowledge.
– *Reported evidentials* are employed if the information comes from a speech report by someone else.

The following examples illustrate five real-life situations. Evidentials were straightforwardly used to express different information sources for the speaker (from author's fieldwork, 2012). (Chicken is expensive and is prized as 'prestige food', so the comments were made in the context of showing how rich and corrupt the uncle was.)

THE WEB OF KNOWLEDGE

(6) Nu-nami karaka di-merita-*naka* Tariana
    1sg-father's.younger.brother chicken 3sgnf-fry-PRESENT.VISUAL
    'My younger uncle is frying chicken' (I (the speaker) see him)

(7) Nu-nami karaka di-merita-*mha*
    1sg-father's.younger.brother chicken 3sgnf-fry-PRESENT.NONVISUAL
    'My younger uncle is frying chicken' (I smell the fried chicken, but cannot see this)

(8) Nu-nami karaka di-merita-*nihka*
    1sg-father's.younger.brother chicken 3sgnf-fry-RECENT.PAST.INFERRED
    'My younger uncle has fried chicken' (I see bits of grease stuck on his hands and he smells of fried chicken)

(9) Nu-nami karaka di-merita-*sika*
    1sg-father's.younger.brother chicken 3sgnf-fry-RECENT.PAST.ASSUMED
    'My younger uncle has fried chicken' (I assume so: he gets so much money he can afford it, and he looks like he has had a nice meal)

(10) Nu-nami karaka di-merita-*pidaka*
    1sg-father's.younger.brother chicken 3sgnf-fry-RECENT.PAST.REPORTED
    'My younger uncle has fried chicken' (I was told recently)

The speaker is likely to have access to more than one information source at the same time. If you see something, you may very well hear it as well, smell it, have enough visual evidence to make an inference, and so on. In general, visually obtained information, if available, is preferred over any other, competing, information source. Barnes (1984: 262) reported the same principle for Tuyuca, an East Tukanoan language spoken in the Colombian part of Vaupés River Basin linguistic area. The next preferred choice will be nonvisual evidential, then inferred based on visible results, then reported, and only then the assumed. These preferences outlined in Scheme 1 reflect the choices one would tend to make if more than one information source is available.

VISUAL < NONVISUAL < INFERRED < REPORTED < ASSUMED

SCHEME 1 Hierarchy of preferred evidentials in Tariana: a general tendency

However, this scheme offers nothing but a general indication of what one might expect. The actual choice of preferred information source will be complicated by a number of further parameters, including
(a) what kind of access speaker has to information,
(b) the type of information, and
(c) the status of the speaker within the community.

For instance, no matter whether or not one sees the shaman perform his duties, the appropriate way will be to talk about them using a nonvisual evidential. Shamanic dreams are cast in visual evidential. In contrast, a dream by a common mortal will always be treated as 'nonvisual' – casting it in visual evidential would either imply that the speaker is not quite competent or that they betray special powers and their dream has a prophetic and thus supernatural quality. The actual choice of evidentials is embedded within the Tariana system of beliefs and attitudes to knowledge. Preferences which govern these choices are intrinsically linked with access to knowledge and can be manipulated in natural discourse to reflect speakers' stance, attitudes, and even societal changes.[7] We return to these issues in section 4.

Recurrent semantic parameters grammaticalised within evidentiality systems are summarised in Scheme 2.

I. VISUAL covering information acquired through seeing.

II. SENSORY covering information acquired through hearing, and is typically extended to smell and taste, and sometimes also touch.

III. INFERENCE based on visible or tangible evidence, or visible results.

IV. ASSUMPTION based on reasoning and conjecture (and not on visible results).

V. REPORTED, for reported information with no reference to who it was reported by.

VI. QUOTATIVE, for reported information with an overt reference to the quoted source.

SCHEME 2   Recurrent meanings in evidential systems

---

7 The hierarchy of preferred evidential choice has been sometimes interpreted as 'best evidence' (for instance, by Matthewson 2004 and further formalist-minded researchers). Such terminology has to be taken with a grain of salt: it implies an intrinsic evaluation of sources stemming from a deductive stance taken by a formalist researcher rather than from a language-internal perspective (see further discussion in Aikhenvald 2018a: 27). Neither does evidentiality come in 'degrees': as shown in Aikhenvald (2004: 6–8), it makes little sense to

There may be further differentiations within these groups of meanings (see also the discussion in Aikhenvald 2004: 59). These include degrees of verbal report. For instance, Mamaindê, a Nambikwara language from southern Amazonia in Brazil, distinguishes secondhand and thirdhand reported evidentials (Eberhard 2018: 337–41). Tatuyo, an East Tukanoan language from the Vaupés River Basin linguistic area in Colombia, distinguishes between two kinds of visual evidential – a simple visual and a distal visual (used to describe something seen from afar) (Stenzel and Gomez-Imbert 2018: 365). A similar distinction between a distant visual and a proximal visual evidential with noun phrase scope has been identified in Lakondê, a Nambikwara language (Eberhard 2018: 345; Telles and Wetzels 2006: 248–9). An evidential referring to visually acquired information (or a 'firsthand' evidential, depending on the system) may be formally unmarked, or less marked than others. A reported evidential may be unlike others in terms of its origins and capacity to combine with other terms (further details are in Aikhenvald 2018a: 15–16).

•••

Table 1 summarises the evidentiality systems with two, three, four and five choices attested in more than one language (adapted from Aikhenvald 2018a: 15; see also discussion there). Each is accompanied with a letter and a number, following the conventions adopted in Aikhenvald (2004: xxiv and 2018a): systems with two choices are referred to with the letter A and a number; systems with three choices with the letter B and a number and so on.

As we will see in section 3, the scope of evidentiality is typically a clause, or a sentence. Alternatively, a noun phrase can have its own information source, and thus fall within the scope of an evidential, with a different information source of the clause or the sentence. Non-propositional evidentiality (discussed, inter alia, in Jacques 2018) is the focus of section 3.1.4. Further special features of evidentiality which set it apart from other categories are discussed in section 3.2–6.

In each instance, evidentials vary as to how obligatory they are. In Kamaiurá, a Tupí-Guaraní language, one may perhaps omit a marker of information source; but a sentence without evidentiality markers will come out as unnatural, 'something artificial, sterile, deprived of colour' (Seki 2000: 347; my translation). In the languages of the Vaupés River Basin linguistic area, including Tariana, omitting an evidential fused with tense will result in an ungrammatical sentence, casting doubt on the speaker's capacity to articulate their speech in an appropriate fashion.

---

talk about 'strong' and 'weak' evidentiality – just like no-one would talk about 'strong' or 'weak' tense or aspect.

TABLE 1 The grouping of semantic parameters in evidentiality systems

		I. Visual	II. Nonvisual sensory	III. Inference	IV. Assumption	V. Reported	VI. Quotative
2 choices	A1	firsthand		non-firsthand			
	A1	firsthand		non-firsthand			
	A2	<evidentially unmarked>		non-firsthand			
	A3	<evidentially unmarked>				reported	
	A4	<evidentially unmarked>	auditory	<evidentially unmarked>			
3 choices	B1	direct		inferred		reported	
	B2	visual	nonvisual	inferred			
	B3	visual	nonvisual	<no term>		reported	
	B4	<evidentially unmarked>	nonvisual	inferred		reported	
	B5	<evidentially unmarked>				reported	quotative
	B6	<evidentially unmarked>	nonvisual	<evidentially unmarked>		reported	
4 choices	C1	visual	nonvisual	inferred		reported	
	C2	direct (or experiential)		inferred	assumed	reported	
	C3	direct (or experiential)		inferred		reported	quotative
	C4	visual	nonvisual	inferred		<evidentially unmarked>	
	C5	direct	inferred		assumed	<evidentially unmarked>	
	C6	<evidentially unmarked>		inferred		reported	quotative
5 choices	D1	visual	nonvisual	inferred	assumed	reported	

1.2 *Egophoricity: Grammatical Expression of Access to Knowledge*

Egophoricity expresses speaker's personal involvement in the action and privileged access to information. The essence of egophoricity in Tibetic languages has been captured by DeLancey (2018: 584), as 'a fundamental distinction between a set of forms which report information to which the speaker has privileged access [...] and those which report information which the speaker finds in the world outside'. This opposition is fundamental to the verbal system of most Tibetic languages. This is how Sun (1993: 955–6) put it:

> In Tibetan, the category of person constitutes an important factor which determines much of the verbal morpho-syntax. The relevant oppositions, however, are not the well-known trichotomy of first person (speaker), second person (interlocutor) and third person (other referents), but rather a referentially fluid dichotomous distinction between self-person and

other person. In rather vague terms, self-person sentences are marked as utterances produced by oneself.

In Munya, a Tibeto-Burman language, the egophoric auxiliary *ŋo* denotes the subject's control and awareness of their action, or their involvement in a given situation. In (11), the auxiliary is used with the first person subject in statements which involve volitional predicates. It cannot be used with those predicates which indicate non-controllable states (Bai 2020: 245–7). The egophoric auxiliary is in italics.

(11) Nɯ   ndö   *ŋo*   *Munya*
     1sg   go/1sg   EGO:SAP
     'I am leaving'

In (12a), the egophoric auxiliary is used in a question addressed to a second person.

(12a) pintçilin   ɛ-ɛ-ndzɛ   *ŋo*   *Munya*
      icecream   DIRN-INTER-eat/2sg   EGO:SAP
      'Do you (want to) eat icecream?'

In (12b), the egophoric auxiliary appears in an embedded clause where the subject is coreferential with that of the matrix clause. The embedded clause is in square brackets.

(12b) ŋuní   [húndzə   ɛ-ndzə   ré   *Munya*
      1pl.EXCL.ERG dinner   DS-eat   go/1/2nonsg
      ɛ-ŋo]Embedded clause   sɔ   pe   nyi
      INTER-EGO:SAP   think   IMPF/1/2nonsg   CONTROL
      'We are thinking whether we should go eat dinner or not'

When the egophoric auxiliary occurs with second person in a declarative clause, it indicates the speaker's privileged access to knowledge. Example (13) can be used if the addressee forgot whether or not she had already had dinner and asks the speaker about it. The speaker will reply (13).

(13) nɛ   i   ɛ-ndzü   *ŋo*   *Munya*
     2sg   ERG   DS-eat/2sg   EGO:SAP
     'You have already eaten/had your meal' (I know it, and you do not)

Using the egophoric -ŋo indicates that the speaker knows something that addressee does not.

These examples illustrate a common pattern for the egophoric marker: first person in statements, second person in questions, and in embedded clauses where the subject of the main clause is coreferential with that of the matrix clause (see Bai 2020: 241–45, DeLancey 2018, Hyslop 2014a, 2018a,b, Sun 2018, and Hargreaves 2018[8]). In earlier work this was referred to with the labels 'conjunct' vs. 'disjunct' person marking (or 'locutor/non-locutor') (see also Dixon 2010b: 222–3). This binary terminological distinction is now considered obsolete, since it reflects a formal opposition rather than its semantic basis.

We will see, in section 4, that some evidentials may have connotations of privileged access to knowledge, and can thus be considered 'egophoric strategies'. The existence of other egophoric strategies attested cross-linguistically is a matter for further research.

1.3 Mirativity: Grammatical Expectations of Knowledge

The range of meanings of mirativity subsume unexpected knowledge and surprise, sudden discovery and unprepared mind, with additional overtones of new information and counterexpectation. The concept of mirativity is a relatively recent arrival on the linguistic scene. It was first defined, by DeLancey (1997), as 'conveying information which is new or unexpected to the speaker', with overtones of surprise. A comparable range of meanings was first described in a grammar of Albanian written in French by Dozon (1879: 226–7) (see Friedman 2003: 192–3, 213, 2010, and 2012, for the history and the meanings of the term). A verb form with 'admirative' meanings was described in a number of grammars of North-East Caucasian languages (e.g. Kibrik 1977, 1994). Many grammars of Quechua languages describe a verb form with a major meaning of 'sudden realization or awareness' and 'surprise' (Adelaar 1977, 2013).

The overtones of 'surprise', and 'new and unexpected information' are characteristic of other categories, including exclamatives, and some evidentials in some systems. In his seminal work, DeLancey (1997, 2001) put 'mirativity' on

---

8 See Sun (2018: 18), and Bai (2020: 241–2), for a summary of reasons for the rejection of the notion of 'conjunct/disjunct' and further references. A somewhat different approach is found in Tournadre and Jiatso (2001) and the work by their followers who tend to confuse evidentiality and egophoricity.

the map as a separate linguistic category. In DeLancey's (2001: 370)'s words, prior to this, mirative constructions were considered 'simply an odd appendage to evidentiality'. There is now enough evidence to show that evidentiality and mirativity are different categories (see DeLancey 1997, 2001, 2012, Hyslop 2018a,b, Aikhenvald 2012, and references therein).

The range of mirative meanings subsumes the following values:

(I) sudden discovery, sudden revelation or realization (a) by the speaker; (b) the audience (or addressee), or (c) by the main character;
(II) surprise (a) of the speaker; (b) of the audience (or addressee), or (c) of the main character;
(III) unprepared mind (a) of the speaker; (b) of the audience (or addressee), or (c) of the main character;
(IV) counter-expectation (a) to the speaker, (b) to the addressee, or (c) to the main character;
(V) information new (a) to the speaker, (b) to the addressee, or (c) to the main character.

An example of a mirative in Munya is in (14) (Bai 2020: 150). The speaker realised that, to her surprise, noodles sprinkled with vinegar were delicious:

(14) reré thoŋósə   *Munya*
   delicious MIR
   'It is delicious!'

A mirative can combine with an evidential. In (15), from Tarma Quechua, the mirative, or 'sudden discovery', marker reflects the information which is new and unexpected to the audience of a story about a race between toads and a deer. The story is cast in reported evidential (as it is 'derived from hearsay': Adelaar 2013: 103).

(15) Rachak-*shi* kinra-n kinra-n   *Tarma Quechua*
   toad-REP side-3POSS side-3POSS
   ĉura-naka-ra-:ri-*na[q]*   ĉaski-yubay-si
   place-RECIP-PERF-PL-3A/S.MIR relay.runner-COMPAR-ADD
   'The toads had posted each other on different spots along the track as in a relay-race.'

Both the reported evidential and the mirative marker are clitics. In this sentence they appear on different constituents within a clause, notwithstanding their clausal scope.

The array of meanings subsumed under the notion of 'mirativity' can be expressed independently, or through other categories, and also through lexical means. In a number of languages, different meanings within the mirative range are realized differently. This alerts us to the fact that 'mirativity' is best applied as a category for which individual values have to be identified. When we describe a linguistic category – be it aspect, or tense, or gender, or evidentiality – we do not just say that a language has 'tense': we specify that it has present, past, and remote past; or past versus non-past. Along similar lines, it is not enough to say that a language has 'mirativity': in each instance, one needs to specify the subset of the range of mirative meanings grammaticalised in the language.

1.4   Epistemic Modality: Grammatical Expression of Attitude to Knowledge

Epistemic modality reflects speaker's assessment of the truth of a statement and their subjective evaluation of the degree of certainty, such as being probable or possible (see a recent summary in Wiemer 2018, papers in Nuyts and van der Auwera 2015 and references there). That epistemic modality and evidentiality are completely different categories is now an established fact (see the summary in Aikhenvald 2004: 258–9, 2018a; pace Palmer 1986 and some later sources, many of them European-oriented and guided by translations into European languages rather than the facts of languages themselves).

Within a given language, evidentials can be semantically complex. The reported evidentials in some (including Estonian, as shown in (29)), may have additional epistemic overtones of unreliable information. In others – including Shipibo-Konibo, Tariana, and Jarawara – they do not. A marker of an epistemic modality may then accompany an evidential. In (16), from Tariana, the marker -*da*, an exponent of dubitative modality, occurs together with a visual evidential and the frustrative modality.

The modal marker -*da* indicates the speaker's uncertainty about the correct use of the Portuguese word 'paleto' (overcoat), with overtones of frustration over the fact that he is not sure of whether the Portuguese word he had seen others using is the right one (see also Aikhenvald 2003a: 387–90).

(16) nha   yalana   na-ña-mi-maka-pe   nha   paleto
      they   white.people   3pl-wear-NOMIN-CL:CLOTH-PL   they   'paleto'
      na:-tha-*ka*-da
      3pl+say-FRUSTRATIVE-REC.P.VIS-DUBITATIVE
      'What white people wear, they are probably the ones (seen by me) called "paleto".'

An evidential and a modal can occur together on one verbal word in Abkhaz, and Hupda (see more examples in Aikhenvald 2004: 258–9).

When telling a story about evil spirits or mythical creatures, a speaker of Tatuyo, an East Tukanoan language, will use 'the reported evidential in conjunction with the epistemic 'stabilizer prefix' *ká-*, indicating that he or she has learned the story indirectly through others and vouches for it' (Stenzel and Gomez-Imbert 2018: 383). The reported evidential and the prefix *ká-* do different jobs: one is an evidential marker of information source, and the other is an exponent of commitment, with an epistemic meaning.

Assumed and inferred evidentials are often translated into English, or Spanish, using epistemic adverbs. As Nuckolls (2018: 205) put it, with regard to the reported evidential *-shi* in Pastaza Quichua, 'despite fact that a *-shi* statement indicates that someone else's knowledge underlies the assertion, there is not necessarily any implication that the statement is unreliable'. Further on, 'whether or not one is committed to what one asserts ... is a matter of epistemic modality', while evidentiality proper reflects the information source and the speaker's 'perspective on knowledge', that is, how they obtained it. We return to this in section 5.

• • •

The four groups of categories related to knowledge, I–IV, interact with each other. Diagram 1 summarises the interactions between their meanings.

This division of knowledge-related categories was in part proposed and elaborated by Hyslop (2014a,b, 2016, 2018a,b) with a focus on Kurtöp and other

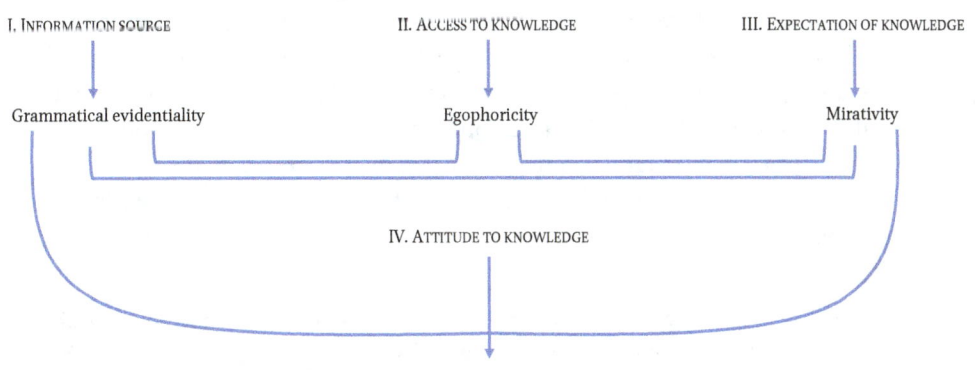

DIAGRAM 1 Evidentiality and other categories related to knowledge

Bodish languages (more on this in Aikhenvald 2018a: 24–7).[9] Further categories potentially related to the expression of knowledge and a few additional issues are addressed in the Appendix.

The solid arrows indicate the core meaning of a category. That one category may have meaning overtones of another one is reflected in lines connecting them. In such cases, one category is used as a 'strategy' to express some meanings which are core to another one. For instance, an epistemic modality can acquire evidential overtones and be deployed as 'evidentiality strategy'.

One of the issues in the analysis of grammatical expression of knowledge, especially with regard to Tibeto-Burman languages and some languages of New Guinea, is a tendency to confuse these four – oftentimes due to the links between them in terms of their expression. As Hyslop (2018b: 595) put it, 'when addressing 'evidentiality' in Bodic languages, specialists of Tibeto-Burman languages tend to include phenomena which are not strictly encoding grammaticalised source of knowledge; expression of knowledge and access to knowledge are notoriously difficult to tease apart from source of knowledge'. Some Tibeto-Burman-focused linguists still tend to treat evidentiality as a 'handmaid' of egophoricity (see, for instance, Hill and Gawne 2017). The concept of 'mirativity' came under attack by Hill (2012). Papers within the same journal issue (especially DeLancey 2012, Friedman 2012, and Aikhenvald 2012) re-established the validity of the category – stressing the point that mirative extensions of other categories, such as evidentiality, can in no way be used as arguments against the existence of mirativity as such.

To reiterate: The four groups of categories (I–IV) are interconnected. Some take on the meanings of the others, as their additional extensions. Throughout the history of studies of each of the groups of categories, the presence of these extensions has created a degree of confusion, depending on the perspective of the researcher. European-focused linguists (starting with Palmer 1986), and linguists with limited experience in non-European languages, lumped evidentiality together with modality. This confusion was based on epistemic extensions of some evidentials in some languages (see section 2.2, and a discussion of flawed approaches and fieldwork methodologies based on translation in section 5).

---

9   In recent years, there has been some confusion between the domains of evidentiality, egophoricity and epistemic modality. Referring to evidentiality and egophoricity as 'epistemic' obliterates the distinction between the accepted terms creating terminological havoc (as done in Widmer 2017, or Hill and Gawne 2017; see Bai 2020: 241–5 for an analysis, and the criticism of uninformed approaches to evidentiality in Aikhenvald (2004: 5–6, 2014, 2018). Chung and Timberlake (1985: 244–6) correctly categorise evidentiality as an 'epistemological mode' to do with information source, using the term 'epistemology' in its conventional, philosophical meaning as defined by Bullock and Stallybrass (1988: 279).

Meanings related to information source appear to be particularly versatile. They can be expressed through other categories, as their additional meanings, or 'side effects'. This is the essence of 'evidentiality strategies' (discussed at length in Aikhenvald 2004, 2014, and in the sources mentioned there). Aspects (especially perfective), tense, reality status, mood, speech reports, nominalizations, and complementation strategies often develop meanings related to information source. In the course of time, they may evolve into dedicated markers of evidentiality (see, for example, a recent discussion of Evenki, a Tungusic language, by Greed 2018a). Note that within multiterm evidential systems, one or two terms may display an epistemic or an egophoric extension. Such extensions never cover every evidential term in a large system: in other words, some but not all evidential terms in a larger system will develop additional meanings.

In section 2, we turn to some examples of semantic links and overlaps between the four groups of categories I–IV. Evidentials stand apart from the other three groups of categories related to knowledge – egophoricity, mirativity, and epistemic modality – in terms of a number of features: this is the topic of section 3. In section 4, we turn to the ways in which semantically complex evidentials may expand into the domain of egophoricity – access to information source and sharing information. Evidentiality and epistemic modality display asymmetrical relations – the topic of section 5.

2 Links between the Four Groups of Grammatical Categories Related to Knowledge

Table 2 summarises the attested examples of links between the four groups of grammatical categories (I–IV). Links for which no examples have been found are accompanied with a question mark.

TABLE 2 Links between the four groups of grammatical categories related to knowledge

From to	I. Evidentiality	II. Egophoricity	III. Mirativity	IV. Epistemic modality
I. Evidentiality	–	A	C	B
II. Egophoricity	D	–	F	E
III. Mirativity	–	–	–	–
IV. Epistemic modality	G	H	–	–

In each instance, an extension of one category into another can be considered a 'strategy' for expressing the meaning associated with the main category. For instance, evidential extensions for markers of epistemic modality or egophoricity can be, and have been, considered 'evidentiality strategies'. For instance, in (43), from Lhasa Tibetan, a marker of personal knowledge has an overtone of direct perception as the information source for the statement. Similarly, a marker of evidentiality which has modal extensions can be considered an 'epistemic modality strategy', as in (21), from Wanka Quechua, (28), from Shipibo-Konibo, and (29), from Estonian.

2.1   Evidentiality → Egophoricity

Grammatical evidentials may reflect privileged access to information source, that is, they can extend into the semantic domain of egophoricity. Verbs referring to internal physical and mental states often require nonvisual evidentials with first person subject, and a different evidential with other persons. This reflects speaker's access to information source and is also known as 'first person effect' in evidentials[10] (see Aikhenvald 2014: 30–1, 2018: 26–7, and Sun 2018: 56–7 for further discussion and references).

In (17), a speaker of Tariana (an Arawak language from Brazil) comments on her own state of being dizzy (during a day of heavy drinking), using the nonvisual evidential. The speaker later explained this usage to me saying 'only I can feel this'.

(17) Yali-*mha*-niki   nu-na   *Tariana*
      be.dizzy-PRES.NONVIS-COMPL   1sg-OBJ
      'I am dizzy' (lit. dizzy to me).

In (18), the speaker talks about his companions whom he had seen being taken with fever. He uses visual evidential, as they were visibly sick.

(18) Na-na-pita   adaki   dhipa-*na*-pita   *Tariana*
      3pl-OBJ-AGAIN   fever   3sgnf+get-REM.P.VIS-AGAIN
      'Fever got them again'

The nonvisual evidential would not be acceptable here because, in the speaker's own words, 'one cannot feel what others feel'. Similar examples are found in

---

10   The term 'first person effect in evidentials' was first used in the position paper for the International Workshop on 'Evidentiality' (published as Aikhenvald 2003b and circulated in the late 2000). Curnow (2002: 180) used the term without referring to the original source in his paper did not make it into the published volume (Aikhenvald and Dixon 2003).

numerous languages with large evidential systems (see, for instance, Eberhard 2018: 349–50 on the use of nonvisual evidential in Mamaindê to indicate one's internal states and feelings).

A nonvisual or indirect evidential with first person subject implies 'reduced access to information', covering accidental action, and lack of control or awareness (see also Sun 2018: 57–8). This is a feature of numerous languages with evidentiality across the world (e.g. Turkic: Johanson 2018: 520, Hinuq: Forker 2014, and also Aikhenvald 2004: 219–232). In (19), a speaker of Tariana broke a ceramic pot accidentally; this is reflected in the choice of nonvisual evidential.

(19) episi-aphi-nuku   nu-thuka-*mahka*   Tariana
     iron-CL:CERAMIC.POT-TOP.NON.A/S 1sg-break-REC.P.NONVIS
     'I broke the pot accidentally'

In (20), the speaker broke the pot on purpose (the speaker commented that it was cracked anyway, and of no use).

(20) episi-aphi-nuku   nu-thuka-*ka*   Tariana
     iron- CL:CERAMIC.POT   1sg-break-REC.P.VIS
     'I broke the pot on purpose'

Extending evidentials to cover access to information can be considered an egophoricity strategy. The extensions are attested in limited grammatical contexts – typically, first person subject and also expressions of physical and mental states (called 'endopathic' within the Tibeto-Burman tradition).

2.2   *Evidentiality → Epistemic Modality*

A grammatical evidential may have additional meanings similar to those associated with epistemic modalities. None of the epistemic extensions of evidentials are universal. The exact semantic content depends on the system, and on the language (a comprehensive analysis is in Aikhenvald 2004: 153–207, and a summary in Aikhenvald 2018a: 16–17; see also the discussion in Wiemer 2018). For each language, it can be shown that modality and evidentiality are different categories. As mentioned above, just a few of evidentials within a multi-term system acquire epistemic extensions – never the whole system.

In a multi-term evidential system, a visual evidential may have overtones of certainty. The direct evidential –*m(i)* in Wanka Quechua may be used this way. In (21), the speaker does not imply that he has seen his parents fail to do a particular job. What it implies is that the speaker is sure that his parents are unable to do it (Floyd 1999: 69–70).

(21) papaa-kaa-si   mana-*m*   atipa-n-chu   *Wanka Quechua*
     father-DEF-also not-DIR.EV   be.able-3p-NEG
     lula-y-ta
     do-IMPF-ACC
     'Our parents can't do it either.'

Similar examples from other Quechua languages are in Nuckolls (1993), on Pastaza Quichua, Adelaar (1977: 79) on Tarma Quechua, Weber (1989: 422ff) on Huallaga Quechua, and Grzech (2016) on Tena Kichwa. Along similar lines, visual evidential in Mamaindê, a Nambikwara language, may acquire overtones of certainty (Eberhard 2018: 349).

Information acquired through vision – or through someone's direct experience – tends to be considered the most reliable, and the most certain. Epistemic overtones of visual, firsthand, or direct evidentials can be interpreted as 'common-sense' implicatures: if I had seen it, it must be certain, and true. Incidentally, such implicatures bear a strong similarity to what Frajzyngier (1985: 252) refers to as the inherent meaning of unmarked indicative sentences in a number of languages used to 'express what the speaker wants to convey as truth'. Further discussion of evidentially neutral sentences and implicatures associated with conventional inferences concerning the type of source they could be based on can be found in Wiemer (2018: 94, 107–8).

A non-firsthand, or non-eyewitness, evidential in a two-term system may acquire overtones of information one does not commit to. In Tatar, a Turkic language, the non-eyewitness suffix -*GAn* typically refers to the information which the speaker may have inferred or acquired via speech report.

In Greed's (2014: 74) words, it 'may show the speaker's evaluation of the reliability of information. However, it would usually be strengthened by contextual cues, for example with words expressing uncertainty or doubt'. This suggests that we are dealing with an implicature: the exact appreciation of probability or possibility of the event is left to a contextual interpretation, rather than being part of the meaning of the form.

An example is in (22) (Greed 2014: 86). Here, the modal particle *imeš*, whose first meaning is that of reported information, imparts a nuance of doubt and even of irony to the statement.

(22) Alsu   kilgän   *imeš*   *Tatar*
     Alsu   come:NONFIRSTH   REP
     'It has been said that Alsu has come' (but the speaker does not really believe it)

In Cree/Montagnais/Naskapi, an Algonquian language, the non-firsthand evidential can be used if the speaker simply chooses to describe the state of affairs as if they were not direct witness of it (even if in fact they were), to make sure the audience understands that they have little to do with the whole thing and are unsure of what had actually happened. (23), from Cree/Montagnais/Naskapi, is an answer to a question: 'What did Sister (a nun) say to you?' (James, Clarke and MacKenzie 2001: 240–3).

(23) tshetshishkutama:shuin nititiku-*shapan*   *Cree/Montagnais/Naskapi*
you.go.to.school   she.told.me-NONFIRSTH
'I think she told me to go to school'

The speaker here is talking about an incident in which she took part. She ought to have had firsthand knowledge of it. The thing is, she does not remember exactly what Sister had said. Choosing not to present oneself as a direct witness is a stylistic option for talking about something one is unsure of. The non-firsthand evidential here has an epistemic connotation: 'she may have told me to go to school, but I am not sure'. It is the context which helps impart epistemic connotations to the non-firsthand evidential.

In a multiterm evidential system, a nonvisual evidential may acquire contextual epistemic overtones of uncertainty. In daily interactions, the nonvisual evidential in Tariana is often used to refer to someone far away whose actions are not seen. The actual overtone of uncertainty is largely contextual. In (24a), Jovino Brito had seen his wife Gloria leave for Manaus, and used the visual evidential to describe this. He cannot see her being in Manaus visiting their children – hence the nonvisual evidential.

(24) Nu-sa-do   Gloria-mia   Manus-*ka*   *Tariana*
     1sg-spouse-fem.sg Gloria-only   Manaus-REC.P.VIS
     du-a   duha
     3sgf-go   she
     du-enipe   alipa-se-*mha*   ikasupiaka-nuku,
     3sgf-children   towards-LOC/ALL-PRES.NONVIS   right.now-TOP.NON.A/S
     ne   Manause-*mha*   du-a
     so   Manaus-PRES.NONVIS   3sgf-go
     'Only my wife Gloria has gone to Manaus (visual), right now to her children she went (nonvisual), to Manaus she went (nonvisual)'.

In a WhatsApp voice message to me, Jovino Brito was worried if I got sick (he was aware of the pressure I had been under). He phrased it using the nonvisual evidential – he could not see me, and there was a tinge of uncertainty as to my state of health (he refers to me as an older sister, according to the kinship system into which I have been adopted).

(25) Du-kamia-ka-*mha*   nu-phe-ru   *Tariana*
     3sgf-fall.ill-DECL-PRES.NONVIS   1sg-older.sibling-FEM.SG
     'My older sister has fallen ill' (nonvisual; implication is that I cannot see her and this may be the case)

Similarly, in another WhatsApp message, Olívia Brito quotes herself as saying 'My adult younger sister died-nonvisual' (referring to me, in agreement with the kinship relationship we are in). She presents herself as being worried about me, as she hadn't heard from me for a day. Her own act of thinking is cast in visual evidential.

(26) nu-we-do-peru   *Tariana*
     1sg-younger.sibling-FEM.SG-ADULT
     du-ñami-ka-*mhana*,
     3sgf-die-DECL-REM.P.NONVIS
     nu-a-*naka*   nu-awada   pi-na
     1sg-say-PRES.VIS   1sg-think   2sg-OBJ
     'My younger sister had died (nonvisual), I am saying thinking about you'

Using a nonvisual evidential to refer to the feelings and internal states by a close relative is also a mark of empathy – as if one 'feels' something a close person is experiencing as if it were one's own feeling (similar to the use of the nonvisual evidential in (17): more on this in Aikhenvald 2021c).

A nonvisual evidential may describe something one cannot really discern very well, and thus may not be sure of and cannot quite make out who it is. A man lost his way while hunting and had to spend the night in the jungle. He then climbed a tree to keep away from jaguars, and said (27). The statement – a direct speech report expressing internal thought – is accompanied with the epistemic adverb *pa:pe* 'maybe', strengthening the epistemic meaning easily derived from the context of the story. The story itself is cast in the remote past evidential, hence the form *-pidana* on last clause.

(27) Pa:pe   di-ni-kayami   yawi   di-wapa-*mha*   *Tariana*
     maybe   3sgnf-do-SEQ   jaguar   3sgnf-wait-PRES.NONVIS
     nu-na   di-a-*pidana*   ka:-kale
     1sg-OBJ   3sgnf-say-REM.P.REP   REL-heart
     'Maybe the jaguar is waiting for me (nonvisual), he said (reported) in his heart'

In the dark of the night, the speaker could not see whether the jaguar was there or not (it came to haunt him later); so the nonvisual evidential has strong overtones of uncertainty. The main line of the story is cast in reported evidential – we return to this in section 4.3.

In a multiterm evidential system of Shipibo-Konibo, a Panoan language from Peru, every term – except the reported – may be used with an epistemic overtone: the direct evidential -*ra* 'extends to certainty', -*bira* 'inferred' extends to probability, and -*mein* 'speculative' to doubt (Valenzuela 2003: 35, 49, 57). An example with the speculative evidential is in (28).

(28) ka-*mein*-ke   Charo   Mashi-nko   *Shipibo-Konibo*
     go-SPECL-COMPL   Charo   Mashi-ALL
     'S/he may have gone to Charo Mashi'

A reported evidential may have overtones of something one does not vouch for. This is typical for small systems which distinguish either direct versus indirect evidentials, or reported versus everything else. An example from Estonian is in (29).

(29) tema   ole-*vat*   arst   *Estonian*
     s/he   be-REP   doctor
     'He is reported to be a doctor' (but I don't vouch for it)

Epistemic extensions of uncertainty are a feature of the quotative evidential in Bashkir, a Turkic language with a witnessed versus a non-witnessed distinctions in the verbal system. This is in addition to reported and quotative evidentiality expressed through particles (see Greed 2018b on these and other extensions of the quotative marker, depending on the context).

Mamaindê, a Nambikwara language, has six evidentials – visual, nonvisual, inferred, general knowledge, and two reported ones: secondhand and thirdhand (we return to this in section 4.1). Both reported specifications have overtones of doubt (Eberhard 2018: 349). This does not mean that a reported evidential will always have a meaning of something one does not trust. In Shipibo-Konibo, with four evidentials, the reported term 'does not indicate uncertainty or a lesser degree of reliability but simply reported information' (Valenzuela 2003: 57). Commitment to the veracity of the utterance will be expressed with other means; a reported evidential does not have any epistemic connotations.

2.3   Evidentiality → Mirativity

In many languages of the world, evidentials have mirative extensions of surprise and unprepared mind, overlapping with the central semantic features of mirativity (Aikhenvald 2004, 2012: 465ff, 2018, Dixon 2004: 203–6). A speaker of Jarawara saw a dead sloth – he was surprised that the sloth was dead, and used the non-firsthand evidential, in (30), despite the fact that he actually saw it (Dixon 2003: 171).

(30) jo   abohi   *Jarawara*
      sloth(masc)   be.dead+COMPL.CL
      home-*hino*
      lie-IMMEDIATE.PAST.NON.FIRSTHAND.MASC
      'A dead sloth lay (there)' (non-firsthand: as a marker of surprise)

Which evidentials would tend to have mirative extensions depends on the structure of the evidential system, and the number, and semantics, of the terms within it. In small evidential systems, with firsthand (or eyewitness) evidential versus non-firsthand (or non-eyewitness) evidential, the non-firsthand term typically acquires mirative meanings, especially in combination with first person (as in examples from Turkish, based on Slobin and Aksu-Koç 1982, Aksu-Koç and Slobin 1986). Many languages employ non-firsthand evidentials, to convey surprise and sudden realization, just like Jarawara does.

Mapudungun, an isolate spoken in the Andean areas of Chile and west central Argentina, has an evidential marker *-rke-* which has a complex of meanings typical for non-firsthand evidential (Smeets 2007: 246–7, 110, Zúñiga ms). The information in (31) comes from a speech report.

(31) Kuyfi   miyaw-*ürke*-y   mawida   mew   *Mapudungun*
      long.ago   walk-RKE-INDICATIVE   forest   through
      'Long ago s/he wandered through the forest' (it is said)

In (32), the same *-rke-* describes what one has inferred based on what one knows.

(32) weðweð-pe-*rke*-la-y   *Mapudungun*
    crazy-PROXIMITY-RKE-INDICATIVE-3person
    'He must be crazy' (that one, he travelled through all that rain)

This same evidential form, -*rke*-, can express speaker's surprise at something unexpected:

(33) Miyaw-pa-*rke*-ymi   *Mapudungun*
    walk-CISLOCATIVE-RKE-2sgINDICATIVE
    'So you are (around) here! (What a surprise!)'

The non-eyewitness evidential marker -*GAn* in Tatar can have mirative overtones in contexts with a first person participant (Greed 2014: 74). The marker indicates that the speaker was not aware of their state. In (34), a Tatar speaker talks about how she and her daughter were watching Eurovision, using the marker (pronounced as -*gan*-). The speaker was not aware of falling asleep while watching the show, which is why she uses a non-eyewitness evidential to describe her own experience.

(34) Bez   axyryna   qadär   qaryj   *Tatar*
    we   end:POSS   until   watch:CONVB
    al-ma-dy-q,
    be.able-NEG-PAST-1pl
    bez   joqla-*gan*-byz.
    we   sleep-PAST.RES.NONWIT-1pl
    'We were not able to watch till the end, we slept'

The use of the non-eyewitness marker -*GAn* shows that she became aware of her falling asleep only when waking up.

(35) Min   üzem   dä   siz-mä-*gän*-men,   *Tatar*
    I   self:1sg   EMPH   feel-NEG-PAST.RES.NONWIT-1sg
    min   joqlap   kit-*kän*-men.
    I   sleep:CONVB   INCH-PAST.RES.NONWIT-1sg
    'Even I had not felt it, I had fallen asleep'

The marker (pronounced as -*gän*- in the first clause and as -*kän*- in the second clause) reflects speaker's post-factum realization of the fact she had fallen asleep during the show and subsequent surprise.

Unwitnessed past forms in Hinuq, a North-East Caucasian language (Forker 2014: 55), also have mirative overtones in the context of first person subject, especially 'when there is something mysterious or unexplainable in the event'. An example is in (36).

(36) hibayłi-š=no   de   Allahli   c'unzi   Ø-u:-n   *Hinuq*
     there-ABL=and   1sg   Allah.ERG   save   I-do-UNWIT
     'And from there Allah also saved me'.

An overtone of 'surprise' is often linked to the lack of previous knowledge of the speaker. In Archi, another North-East Caucasian language, the non-firsthand marker *li* (Kibrik 1977: 230–31) can be used if the speaker participated in a situation the meaning of which is unknown to the hearer, and turns out to be unexpected for the hearer (see also Forker 2018 for a general perspective on North-East Caucasian languages). Similar examples from North-East Caucasian languages Tsakhur and Khwarshi, and a few other languages with two-term evidentiality systems, including Kalasha, a Dardic language, and Northern Khanty, a Ugric language, are in Aikhenvald (2012: 469).

Along similar lines, in Saaroa, a Formosan language (Pan 2014: 98–9), a reported evidential may imply 'new, unusual and surprising information'. In (37), the reported evidential implies new knowledge and surprise for the speaker: it is unusual to have had a chance to encountered a bear in the mountains.

(37) amilh-a   amalhe=na   lhi-k<um>ita=**ami**   *Saaroa*
     say-PV   male.name=DEF   PERF-see<AV>=EVID
     vuvulungaa   n   cumi'i
     mountain   OBL   bear
     'Amalhe said he saw a bear in the mountain (surprisingly)'

A morpheme, on its way towards evolving into a grammaticalised reported evidential, may develop semantic overtones similar to those of a true reported evidential. The reported particle *dizque* (literally, '(it) says that') in Colombian Spanish is a case in point. An erstwhile marker of reported speech, it developed a variety of meanings associated with non-firsthand information and can also refer to nonvolitional and uncontrollable actions which go against the speaker's expectations (Travis 2006).

An example of this mirative extension is in (38) (Travis 2006). To his disgust, the speaker has been given a job cleaning bathrooms. He lists a number of ways in which he is unsuitable for the job because he is over sensitive to cleanliness. He then expresses his disbelief at finding himself in this position. This is where he uses *dizque*. In this example, *dizque* does not mark reported speech. Rather, it indicates that the speaker has no control over the situation. In Travis's words, 'it also expresses an element of surprise, as though he has all of a sudden found himself in this terrible situation'.

(38) ... yo, que incluso algunas veces limpié la taza   *Colombian Spanish*
      que otro había chapoteado para que quien usara el baño después
      de mí no fuera a pensar que el descarado había sido yo;
      yo, por Dios, *dizque* a limpiar baños
      '... me, who even sometimes wiped the toilet bowl that someone else had splattered so that whoever used the bathroom after me wouldn't think that the shameless one had been me; I, for God's sake, *dizque* to clean bathrooms'

Speakers of Amazonian Portuguese also employ *diz que* 'says that', generally used to transmit reported information, to talk about uncontrolled action, or when they want to distance themselves from what is happening. Franci – normally averse to any household chores – suddenly decided to try and do some cooking. I was surprised, and asked her what she was doing. The answer was *tou fazendo bolinho dizque* 'I am making pancakes it is said'. Here *dizque* appears as a marker of uncontrolled and unusual action – she was not sure of the result (and surprised at her own endeavour; a similar example, from Colombian Spanish, is in Travis 2006: 1292).

In larger evidential systems, mirative overtones tend to be associated with the inferred or the reported term. Washo, a Wakashan language (Jacobsen 1964; 1986: 8), has three evidentials: visual *-iye?*, auditory *-delem* and *-á?yi?* 'inferential' which expresses an 'post-facto inference with some connotation of surprise'. The assumed evidential *-mein* in a four-term system in Shipibo-Konibo may be used when 'the speaker is confused or surprised because what he experiences is totally unexpected or contradicts his knowledge of the world' (Valenzuela 2003: 48). Whether the evidential *-mein* has mirative overtones or not depends on the context. There are a number of other strategies in the language used to mark surprise: they include an emphatic suffix, a contrastive suffix and a periphrastic verb form involving a doubled auxiliary.

In Tsafiki, a Barbacoan language with four evidentials (direct, or eyewitness, inferential, deductive, and reported, or hearsay), the inferential evidential can indicate surprise of the speaker who has made an unexpected discovery (Dickinson 2000: 411). The inferential evidential typically expressed inference based on visible traces of the event. In (39), the speaker hears what he thought was a car approaching. When he saw it, he realises, to his surprise, that this was a motorcycle.

(39) moto   jo-nu-e   *Tsafiki*
     motocycle be-INFR.EVID/MIR-DECL
     'It's a motorcycle!'

The Northern Nambikwara language Mamaindê (spoken in Brazil) has six evidentials: marking what one saw (visual); what one did not see but heard or smelt or tasted (nonvisual); what one inferred based on visual traces or assumption; what belongs to 'general knowledge' (more on this in section 4.1); what one knows as secondhand report and what one knows as thirdhand report. The inferred evidential has mirative extensions, that is, 'the additional function of expressing surprise' (Eberhard 2009: 466–7). An outsider returned to the village after many years of absence and has not forgotten the language. The inferred evidential, -*sihi*)*n*- is used in its 'mirative' function:

(40) wa-sen-na-sao-leʔi-tu   *Mamaindê*
     2SG-speak-1PL-NOUN.CLASS:SOUND-PAST-FINAL.NOMINAL.SUFFIX
     mamãinsa-a-haiʔki
     Mamaindê-GENITIVE-language
     set-thahta-nu-sao-leʔi-tu
     speak-O1.PL-2nd.subject-NOUN.CLASS.SOUND-PAST-FINAL.NOMINAL.SUFFIX
     nakajuannĩn-ʔna-jeʔ-le-Ø-nʔ-*sihĩn*-wa
     forget-2.object-EMPHATIC-1PAST-3rd.subject-NEG-PAST/INFR-DECL
     'Your old speech, the Mamaindê language with which you used to speak to us, you clearly have not forgotten it'

In multiterm evidential systems in Wanano (or Kotiria) and Piratapuya (or Wa'ikhana), two closely related East Tukanoan languages from the Vaupés River Basin linguistic area, mirative meanings are also associated with the assumed or inferential evidential construction (Stenzel and Gomez-Imbert 2018: 371–2). The mirative meanings appear in the context of first person subject. (41), from Wanano, was 'uttered by a long-dead creature who has just been magically revived', 'seemingly coding the creature's great surprise at finding himself awake (alive) again'.

(41) jiʔɨ   ~kharí-jiʔdɨ-a   waʔá-ri   hí-ka   *Wanano*
     1SG   sleep-INTENS-AFFECT   go-NOMIN   COP-ASSUM.IMPERF
     'I've been asleep a long time!'

In (42), the speaker of Piratapuya uses the inferential evidential (etymologically formed by a nominalised copula accompanied by a copula marked with a visual evidential, similar to inferential markers in Tariana and Tucano, spoken in the same area: Aikhenvald 2002: 124). The speaker is saying that getting drunk really wasn't his fault – he just didn't realize he was drinking sweet potato beer, hence the mirative meaning.

(42) ~si'di siti-wiha   wa'a-dɨ ~japi-ko   *Piratapuya*
     drink smell-go.outward go-SG.M sweet.potato-CL:LIQUID
     ihi-*di*   ihi-di
     COP-NOMIN   COP-VIS.PERF.2/3
     'I became drunk (because apparently) it was sweet potato beer'

In each instance, the speaker's surprise comes as a result of 'deferred realization'. This is a post-factum inference made on the basis of something that the speaker had previously witnessed but only later could realise what it had meant. (Note, however, that no mirative overtones of any of these evidentials have been documented for Tariana or Tucano, from the same linguistic area).

'Surprise' does not necessarily depend on the way in which information was acquired. A reported evidential can also acquire connotations of 'surprise' and 'after-the-fact' realization. In his incisive analysis of the use of the reported evidential in Quechua riddles, Floyd (1996: 919) pointed out a link between mirativity and 'after-the-fact' realization. Similar meanings of the reported evidentiality marker *lę́k'eh* in Western Apache, and their overtones to do with speaker's unprepared mind, and surprise based on deferred realization were discussed by de Reuse (2003) (to whom we owe the concept of 'deferred realization').

Scheme 3 summarises a pathway involved in the development of mirative extensions of non-firsthand evidentials.

---

lack of firsthand information → speaker's non-participation and lack of control → unprepared mind and new knowledge → mirative reading

---

SCHEME 3   Mirative extensions of an evidential: a potential pathway

This path explains the frequent link between non-firsthand specification (which may include reported, inferred, or assumed information, depending on the system), on the one hand, and new information and 'unprepared mind' – which are among the core meanings of mirativity – on the other. We have seen in the examples above that mirative overtones are often interconnected with the speaker's lack of control and lack of awareness of what's going on. The 'lack of control' and lack of awareness is a characteristic effect of the use of first person with non-firsthand evidentials in small systems. This is why mirative extensions frequently occur in first person contexts.

An alternative semantic path is shown in Scheme 4.

> (II) Speaker's deliberate non-participation → distancing effect → presenting the information as new, unexpected and thus 'surprising'

SCHEME 4 Mirative extensions of an evidential: an alternative pathway

A deliberate 'distancing' effect of an inferential evidential creates the possibility of presenting information as new and thus 'surprising'. The paths presented in Schemes 3 and 4 are interconnected: the main difference between them is whether the speaker does or does not exercise deliberate distancing or their non-participation.

Scheme 5 involves the concept of 'deferred' realization – whereby the speaker gives a post-factum interpretation to what they may have observed in some way. Deferred realization is an integral part of mirative meanings in all systems where mirativity is associated with inference. Deferred realization does not, however, necessarily imply a mirative reading (Maslova 2003: 224). And it is also possible that in some languages – such as Western Apache (de Reuse 2003), where evidentiality is not a single grammatical category – 'deferred realization' is a special semantic category overlapping with a putative evidential.

> (III) deferred realization: speaker sees or learns the result but interprets it post factum → the newly understood result is unexpected and thus surprising

SCHEME 5 Mirative extensions of an evidential: deferred realization: a further alternative path

'Deferred realization' can be linked to the speaker's surprise at the post-factum interpretation of what one had seen, or heard, or inferred. This interpretation is part of inference based on the erstwhile perception (which does not involve any other information source). None of these paths are unique to any particular evidentiality system.

However, whether 'deferred realization' always has to involve surprise remains an open question. One of the inferential evidentials, -*biw*, in Kashaya (Oswalt 1986: 42) describes events or states perceived by some means and which have become interpretable later – for instance, if a woman saw a man approaching but could not recognize him until he arrived, she could say 'it is-*bɨw* (INFERENTIAL) my husband'. Whether a newly discovered piece of information is indeed surprising may well depend on the context.

Visual or direct evidentials hardly ever have any mirative extensions. Cupeño, a Uto-Aztecan language, may be an exception to this. Hill (2005: 63, 66–9) describes the evidential clitic =(*a*)*m* in Cupeño as a mirative used 'to express that the utterance is based on unimpeachable firsthand knowledge where the speaker is usually speaking in the moment of discovery'. It is in a paradigmatic relationship with the other evidential marker, the reportative =*ku'ut*. In Hill's (2005) analysis, the clitic =(*a*)*m* is both an evidential and a mirative. Cupeño is no longer actively spoken. Hill only turned her attention to mirativity while writing her grammar a long time after her fieldwork had been completed; the grammar was based on texts and notes collected decades ago when Cupeño still had some speakers or rememberers. There is unfortunately no way for the exact status of =(*a*)*m* to be ascertained.

2.4 *Egophoricity → Evidentiality*

Marking access to information may be fully independent of evidentiality. For instance, nDrapa, a Qiangic (Tibeto-Burman) language, has different markers for evidentiality and for mirativity (Shirai 2007: 145–6). Alternatively, the choice of the marker of access to information may correlate with the information source the statement is based on. An egophoric marker may have overtones of visual or direct access to information (Mélac 2019 refers to egophoric forms with overtones of information sources as 'marginally evidential').

An example of the egophoric existential copula *yod* from Lhasa Tibetan is in (43) (DeLancey 2018: 582). This statement can be described as 'expressing personal knowledge', but, in DeLancey's words, is 'perhaps better thought of as self-representation'. The statement expresses 'the speaker's personal view of her place in the world', and can also be understood as based on direct perception, and thus reflect an information source.

(43) nga-'i   nang   bod-la   yod   *Lhasa Tibetan*
      1SG-GEN   home   Tibet-LOC   exist.PERSONAL
      'My home is in Tibet'

Egophoric markers may be mutually exclusive with evidentials (see Sun 2018: 50–1, on Taku; see also Hein 2007, on Tabo Tibetan). Close links between information source and access to information have led some scholars to include egophoric and evidentials in one system (cf. the term 'egophoric evidential perspective' in Watters 2018: 339 on spoken Dzongkha, and also Hill and Gawne 2017).

It can be argued that a visual or a direct evidential presupposes personal access to information on behalf of the speaker, and thus has an in-built overtone of egophoricity. This overtone, however, will not cover all the meanings and uses associated with any of the evidential terms, with their primary meaning of information source.

2.5   Egophoricity → Epistemic Modality

One would expect that an egophoric marker expressing personal access to information source will have epistemic overtones of certainty on behalf of the speaker. Egophoric markers used in perfective aspect in Kurtöp (Hyslop 2014a: 113) have overtones of certainty. Egophoric markers in Munya (Bai 2020: 245–9 and p.c.) have 'epistemic connotations of certainty on behalf of the speaker'. The statement in (44) will be used if the addressee forgot whether she already had dinner or not and asks the speaker about it. The speaker has privileged access to knowledge and is sure of what they are stating.

(44) nɛ!   i   ɛ-ndzü   ŋo   *Munya*
     2sg   ERG   DIRN-eat.2sg   EGO:SAP
     'You have already eaten'

Along similar lines, Watters (2018: 359) suggests that in Dzongkha speaker's perspective as an egophoric category implies certainty. A number of epistemic markers in Lhasa Tibetan may express uncertainty based on 'speaker's subjective feelings or personal commitment', e.g. *-a yod* 'low probability, based on subjective feelings, personal commitment', in contrast to *-yin.gyi. ma.red* 'low probability based on objective evidence', and *-yod-pa-yod* 'uncertainty based on vague personal memories' (Eric Mélac, p.c.). No examples of overtones of uncertainty of purely egophoric marking have been attested elsewhere.

2.6   Egophoricity → Mirativity

In a number of Tibeto-Burman languages the alternation between egophoric and non-egophoric (or 'alterphoric') marking (formerly known as conjunct/disjunct) can mark new information and surprise, especially in first person contexts. Examples come from Lhasa Tibetan, Akha, Chepang and Newari (DeLancey 1997: 44; see also Hyslop 2018a: 117ff, for a comparison between Kurtöp and Tibetan). Similar examples have been found in Tsafiki, a Barbacoan language from Ecuador (Dickinson 2000).

In Tsafiki (Dickinson 2000), egophoric markers are used with 1st person subject in statements and second person subject in questions. (45) is a simple statement, 'I have money'.

(45) kala   ta-yo-e   *Tsafiki*
     money   have-EGOPHORIC/CONJUNCT-DECL
     '(I) have money'

If the speaker suddenly discovers to their surprise they have some money which they did not think they had, the alterphoric (or disjunct) marker would be used:

(46) kala   ta-i̱-e   *Tsafiki*
     money   have-ALTERPHORIC/DISJUNCT-DECL
     '(I) have money!' (what a surprise!)

This mirative effect is produced by a combination of first person speaker and subject with a form which implies lack of personal access. This is similar to the mirative effect of nonvisual or indirect evidentials discussed under C and Scheme 3. In these instances, what would have been regarded as personal access is actually expressed as if it were not.

2.7   *Epistemic Modality → Evidentiality*

Epistemic modalities may develop meanings comparable to non-firsthand evidentials (and can thus be considered evidentiality strategies). One of the best known examples is conditional in French, known as *conditionnel de l'information incertaine* (also known as *conditionnel de l'information hypothétique, conditionnel de la rumeur, conditionnel de l'information prudente*, etc.: see Dendale 1993).

(47) Edward Snowden *aurait* accepté la proposition d'asile   *French*
     du Venezuela
     'Edward Snowden allegedly accepted the proposal of asylum
     to Venezuela' or
     'Edward Snowden may have accepted/appears to have accepted ...'

The conditional in main clauses has the following meanings:
(a) it expresses uncertainty as to the information conveyed;
(b) it indicates that the speaker or the writer takes no responsibility for the information;
(c) it indicates that the information was taken from some other source.

In Aguaruna, a Jivaroan language from Peru, speculative modality may imply assumption and thus have a meaning typically associated with evidentials (Overall 2017: 377–9). A complex predicate with deontic meaning of 'circumstantial necessity' in Buryat, a Mongolic language, may also express general assumption, as shown in (48) (Brosig and Skribnik 2018: 571–2).

(48) Taanar, nügel_edleeše-d, nügel-öö nyüd-öör-öö *Buryat*
 you sinner-PL sin-REFL eye-INS-REFL
 xara-xa bolo-bo geeše-t
 see-PARTIC.FUT AUX-PAST PART-2PL
 'You, sinners, must have come to see your sins with your own eyes'

2.8 *Epistemic Modality → Egophoricity*

A marker of epistemic modality may presuppose personal access to information, or perhaps lack thereof. What is essentially an epistemic modal may have egophoric overtones.

In Maaka, a Chadic language (Storch and Coly 2014: 199–200), the marker -*ntí* indicates speaker's absolute certainty. It is described as an epistemic modal marker which reflects speaker's privileged access to knowledge. This is not a marker of information source, because 'the source of information is irrelevant'. An example is in (49).

(49) ʔìnndá mmù ʔà mìnè-ndéré ɓáyà *Maaka*
 stand:IMP 1du then 1pl-run:NARR otherwise
 mòo-yá-dìyà
 people-DEF-EVID:JOINT:VIS
 ʔà dùkà-*ntí*-mìnê
 then kill:TR-ASSERT-OBJ:1pl
 'Stand up! We both then run, otherwise the people we both see/know will definitely kill us'

The following extensions have not been attested so far:
  ? EPISTEMIC MODALITY → MIRATIVITY
  ? MIRATIVITY → EVIDENTIALITY
  ? MIRATIVITY → EGOPHORICITY
  ? MIRATIVITY → EPISTEMIC MODALITY

All of the unattested types involve mirativity. The issue here may have to do with the broader character of mirativity and the number of interrelated concepts potentially subsumed under the label in the grammatical studies we have access to. As shown in Aikhenvald (2012) and DeLancey (2012), in individual language studies the label 'mirativity' may cover all of counterexpectation, unprepared mind, new information, and focus. The absence of the links listed above may well be due to a liberal application of the term 'mirativity' within individual grammars, and subsequent analytical difficulties., as the concept of 'mirativity' gets extended to subsume a wide variety of meanings.

3 How Evidentials Are Special

Evidentials stand apart from the other three groups of categories (II–IV) based on the following properties –
- their scope (section 3.1);
- the option of their double marking (section 3.2);
- independent time reference (section 3.3);
- their ability to be negated independently (section 3.4);
- the ability to be questioned independently from the predicate (section 3.5);
- correlations between evidentials, speech genres, and social environment (section 3.6).

Interim conclusions are in section 3.7. A summary is in Table 3.

TABLE 3   How evidentials are special

Features		Evidentiality	Epistemic modality	Egophoricity	Mirativity
Scope: section 3.1	NP	possible	possible	no	rare
	clause	yes	yes	no	no
	sentence	yes	yes	yes	yes
	paragraph	possible	possible	no	no
Double marking: section 3.2		possible	possible	no	no
Time reference different from that of the predicate: section 3.3		possible	no	no	no
Can be negated separately from the verb: section 3.4		possible	no	no	no
Can be questioned separately from the verb: section 3.5		possible	no	no	no
Correlations with speech genres and social environment: section 3.6		yes	no	no	no

3.1 The Scope of Evidentials

Evidentiality (I), egophoricity (II), mirativity (III), and epistemic modality (IV) differ in terms of their scope possibilities. The scope of egophoricity is always the full sentence (see Watters 2018 on the how egophoricity cannot have a dependent clause within its scope).

All documented examples of mirativity point in the same direction (Aikhenvald 2012, and examples there). Mirativity has sentential scope independently of where it is marked – whether with a bound morpheme on the verb, or with a sentential particle. Hone, a Jukunoid language from the Benue-Congo family, is unusual: the language marks mirativity in a series of pronouns which show that 'an action was performed unexpectedly, surprisingly or in an unusual manner' (Storch 1999: 136–7; 2009: 133–4, forthcoming). The implication of the Hone mirative pronouns is that a person is performing an action, 'even though s/he was not supposed to do so or was not expected to be capable of it', or was not allowed to do it. Mirative pronouns only occur with verbs in perfective aspect, and have overtones of focus. Mirative pronouns in Wapha, a Jukun language closely related to Hone, 'express an extraordinary and miraculous event that has been accomplished' by the subject (Storch forthcoming, and p.c.)

Chechen and Ingush, Nakh-Daghestanian languages, express what Molochieva and Nichols (2018: 41–7) refer to as 'the status of information' through special forms of dative pronouns. In both languages, the 'addressee dative' pronouns are used if the speaker 'announces something important that is of interest to the hearer, usually something new or unexpected to the hearer, and known to others besides the speaker' (p. 45). Nichols (2011: 280–3) refers to these as 'mirative pronouns'. An example from Ingush is in (50) (Molochieva and Nichols 2018: 45).

(50) Yz   sou   hwalxa   j-y   *hwuona*   *Ingush*
     3sg   too   early   j-be.PRES   2sg.ADDR

'That's too early!' (Speaker knows this better than hearer does. Or the hearer is in a position of authority and has announced an early meeting: speaker argues against the proposed time.)

The first person inclusive pronouns *vaina* in Ingush has an additional, mirative-like meaning. By using *vaina*, 'the speaker states an important generalization or point that is known to both speaker and hearer, but is not in the hearer's immediate consciousness)' (Nichols 2011: 282). This is illustrated in (51) (Nichols 2011: 282, Molochieva and Nichols 2018: 45–6).

(51) Yz   sou   hwalxa   j-y   vaina   *Ingush*
     3sg   too   early   j-be.PRES   1pl.incl.ADDR
     'That's too early!' (The hearer has proposed an early morning meeting.
     S/he might have anticipated this response as both speaker and hearer
     have an interest in the meeting, and/or they are working together to set
     it up.)

The meanings of addressee pronouns in Ingush bear a strong similarity to the meanings subsumed under the concept of mirativity. These, together with mirative pronouns in Hone, could be considered instances of mirativity with non-propositional, or NP, scope.

In Chechen, the dative pronouns are used when the speaker knows that the addressee requires the information: the speaker may be aware of the fact that the information is relevant for the addressee, or they may assume that the addressee may be interested in the information. In (52), the 'speaker is outside and asking his sister (who is inside) to give him his hat. He knows that she does not know where his hat is, and she is interested in this information' (Molochieva and Nichols 2018: 43). The dative pronoun which reflects addressee's interest in the information is in italics.

(52) Waishaat,   sa(n)   kui   hwa-loo-hw   *Chechen*
     Aishat.NOM   1sg.GEN   hat.NOM   here-give-IMP.2sg
     polki   t'iahw   b-u   *hwuun*
     shelf.NOM   on   B.AGREEMENT.CLASS-be.PRES   2sg.ADDR
     'Aishat, give (me) my hat. (It) is on the shelf (for your information)'

Addressee pronouns expressing hearer's interest and involvement are 'widely attested in conversations and dialogues, but rarely in other contexts and never in subordinate clauses or in interrogative clauses'. Their usage and semantic range reflect access to knowledge, and may be interpreted as an egophoricity strategy.

These are the only instances which could be interpreted as mirativity or egophoricity with non-propositional scope. In addition, a demonstrative can be used as a mirative strategy, that is, as a means of expressing surprise and unprepared mind of the speaker. In Manambu, a Ndu language from East Sepik Province of Papua New Guinea, the proximal demonstrative *ke-* 'close to speaker' (unmarked for additional distance) is often used as an interjection expressing surprise. No other demonstratives in the language are used this way (Aikhenvald 2015d: 17). Along similar lines, the visible proximal demonstrative *(o)ro* 'this: visible' in Tiang, an Oceanic language from New Ireland in Papua New Guinea, is the only demonstrative term with emotional overtones of surprise (or even anger) of the speaker (Holz forthcoming).

In contrast, there are recurrent examples of varying scope for evidentials and of epistemic modals. Their scope may be (i) a sentence – see section 3.1.1, (ii) an individual clause within a sentence – see section 3.1.2, (iii) a paragraph – see section 3.1.3, and (iv) an NP – see section 3.1.4.

3.1.1   Evidentials with Sentential Scope

In the majority of languages with evidentiality, evidentials have the whole sentence with its scope (see typological studies in Aikhenvald 2004, 2018, and references there). Examples (6)–(10) from Tariana and (15) from Tarma Quechua illustrate the point. Evidentiality markers in these languages and in Shipibo-Konibo are also clitics – they do not have to attach to the predicate (see Valenzuela 2003: 44, 47). Notwithstanding their position, they have the whole sentence within their scope. Along similar lines, epistemic modal markers typically scope over a whole sentence (see also Wiemer 2018). The same applies to egophoric and mirative markers.

3.1.2   Evidentials with Clausal Scope

Having an individual clause within the scope of an evidential implies that a non-main clause can have an evidentiality value different from that of the main clause. In many languages evidentials can only occur in main clauses (see Aikhenvald 2004: 253–6, and also Fleck 2007). Non-main clauses never have more evidentiality choices than main clauses (see, for instance, the discussion of evidential distinctions in consequence and purposive clauses in Tucano and Tariana in Aikhenvald 2004: 255).

A dependent clause may have its own evidentiality specifications, different from those of the main clause. Jarawara, an Arawá language, distinguishes witnessed and unwitnessed evidentials (expressed within the past only), in addition to a reported evidential. Relative clause is the only dependent clause type in which evidential distinctions are made. An example is in (53) (R. M. W. Dixon, p.c.).

(53) Bamana   [[Tokomisa   fati]$_S$ *Jarawara*
     Bamana   Tokomisa   wife
     ita-*hani*]$_{RC}$
     sit-IMM.PAST.NONEYEWITNESS.FEM
     to-wasi-maki-*mata-mona*-ka
     AWAY-find-FOLLOWING-FAR.PAST.NONEYEWITNESS.MASC-REP.MASC-DECL.MASC
     'Bamana is said to have found, following a long time ago, Tokomisa's wife, who was sitting'

The main clause, 'Bamana is said to have found following a long time ago, Tokomisa's wife', contains reported information; the information about Tokomisa's wife within the relative clause is noneyewitness (rather than reported). Other dependent clauses in the language are 'evidentiality-neutral': they do not allow marking of their own information source (Dixon 2003: 173–4, 2004: 462, 469, 530; see Dixon 2004: 470 for some exceptional cases of dependent clauses with their own evidential marking).

Estonian has a reported evidential in opposition to evidentially neutral forms (an example is in (29)). A reported evidential can occur in dependent clauses, including complement clauses (54) and relative clauses (55) (Skribnik and Kehayov 2018: 535).

(54) Nende   kohta   kirjutas   kroonik   Henrik,   *Estonian*
     they:GEN about   write:PAST.3SG   annalist Henrik,
     et   nad *ole-vat*   *kannatanud*   suurt   eestlaste
     that   they be-REP   suffer:PAST.PARTIC   great:PARTIT   Estonian:PL.GEN
     ja   liivlaste   ülekohut
     and   Livonian:PL.GEN   injustice:PARTIT
     'The annalist Henrik wrote about them that they have suffered under a great injustice from Estonians and Livonians'

(55) Venelased   ja   teisedki   naersid   *Estonian*
     Russian:PL   and   others:ALSO   laugh:PAST.3PL
     eestlaste   üle,
     Estonian:PL.GEN   over
     kes   *taht-vat*   täita   vene   korraldusi   .
     who   want-REP   fulfill.INFIN   Russian   order:PL.PARTIT
     saksa   täpsusega
     German   precision:COM
     'The Russian and the others were laughing at Estonians, who have been said to want to fulfil the Russian orders with German precision'

They can occasionally occur in temporal and factual conditional clauses (Petar Kehayov, p.c.), as shown in (56).

(56) Ei   *taht-vat*   naise-ga   jalutada   *Estonian*
    NEG   want-REP   wife.GEN-COM   walk.INFIN
    ja   kui   *mine-vat*   siis   on   tusane
    and   if/when walk-REP   then   is   silent
    ei   *kõnele-vat*   sõna-gi
    NEG   utter-REP   word-EMPH

'He reportedly didn't want to walk with the wife, and when/if he (reportedly) went, he was silent, (reportedly) did not utter a word'

Along similar lines, in a complex sentence in Bulgarian and in Macedonian, the non-witnessed evidential marker can be used in a complement clause or in a relative clause with just this clause – and not the whole sentence – in its scope (Tania Kuteva, p.c., Victor Friedman 2003, and p.c.). Both Bulgarian and Macedonian have small evidential systems (witnessed versus nonwitnessed). In (57) the relative clause is within the scope of the non-witnessed evidential (Tania Kuteva, p.c.).

(57) Te   presledvaxa   edin   moj   prijatel,   *Bulgarian*
     they   chase.3PL.IMPERFECT   one   my   friend
     kojto   *bil*   *pravel*   saštoto   nešto,
     REL.MASC   be.EVID.MASC   do.IMPF.EVID.MASC   same.DEF   thing
     i   iskaxa   da   go   složat   v   tanka.
     and   want.3PL.IMPERFECT   to   him   put   in   tank.DEF

'They were chasing a friend of mine who was said to be doing the same thing and they wanted me to put him in the tank.'

In Brokpa, a Bodish (Tibeto-Burman) language from Bhutan (Wangdi forthcoming: Chapter 14), a complement clause may have its own evidential specification.

Exponents of epistemic modality can have a clause within their scope, without having their scope over the whole sentence, as in English *I found a word which would have been appropriate in the circumstances*. There are no instances of either egophoric or mirative markers whose scope would include a clause within a sentence, without including the whole sentence.

3.1.3   Evidentials Whose Scope Goes beyond a Sentence

Evidentiality may have a whole paragraph or a sequence of sentences within its scope. This is the case with the hearsay clitic in Eastern Pomo (McLendon 2003: 119–20, 106), and the reported evidential in Baniwa of Içana. Along similar lines, a sentence without an evidential in Quechua can be understood as having the same evidentiality value as other sentences in the same text (Faller 2002: 23). In Shipibo-Konibo the evidential markers do not have to appear in every clause or every sentence. Evidentiality is obligatory 'in the sense that the evidential value of the information has always been grammatically marked in the foregoing discourse and is clear to native speakers' (Valenzuela 2003: 39). Along similar lines, the reported evidential in Baniwa – illustrated in example (2) – can appear on the first sentence of the paragraph, without having to be repeated on every sentence within it. Once the reported evidential is used, the whole paragraph will be within its scope.

No such scope effects have been described for egophoricity, epistemic modality, or mirativity (with a possible exception for mirative pronouns in Hone and Ingush (50)–(51) in section 3.1).

3.1.4   A Noun Phrase within the Scope of an Evidential: Non-propositional Evidentiality

An evidential can have a noun phrase within its scope. Then, the information source concerning the noun phrase can be different from that of the predicate. This phenomenon is known as non-propositional evidentiality (Jacques 2018, Aikhenvald 2014: 18–19, 2015a, Dixon 2014). Systems of non-propositional evidentiality vary.

Evidential distinctions may be expressed just within a noun phrase (see Dixon 2014, on Dyirbal; Carol 2011 on Chorote and Gutiérrez 2015 on Nivaĉle, both Mataco-Mataguayan). Other languages have different evidentiality systems with NP scope and with clausal scope (see Storch and Coly 2014, on Maaka; Lowe 1999, on Southern Nambikwara; and Pan 2018: 68–72, on Tsou).

Jarawara is among the few languages described so far where the same system of evidentiality markers fused with tense applies to NPs and to clauses (cf. (53); Dixon 2004: 306–9; 489). In (58), the speaker was talking about what had happened to him and his companions, using far past tense eyewitness evidential (referring to what had happened more than two years ago): they had seen a place which had been reported to be another group's old village (Dixon, p.c.):

(58) [[mee   tabori   *Jarawara*
      3NSG   home:FEM
      botee]-*mete-moneha*]$_{NP:O}$
      old-FAR.PAST.NONEYEWITNESS.FEM-REP.FEM
      otaa$_A$ awa-*hamaro*   ama-ke
      NSG.EXC   see-FAR.PAST.EYEWITNESS.FEM   EXTENT-DECL.FEM
      'We were seeing in the far past what was reported to be their old camp from far past'

The noun phrase, 'their old camp from far past', is within the scope of a reported evidential. The sentence (and its predicate) is cast in the eyewitness evidential. The speaker used the far past (to reflect that it was some time ago) and a firsthand (or eyewitness) evidential (to reflect that he had been there and had seen everything himself). And he used the non-firsthand version of far past tense plus the reported evidential suffix with the name of the location – reportedly known to have been another group's old village. This is why the old village is marked with reported evidential (another similar example is in Aikhenvald 2004: 88, based on Dixon's p.c.; see also Dixon 2004: 308, and example 10.67 there).

Along similar lines, the reported evidential in Ilonggo, a Philippine language, can have an NP as its scope (Daguman 2018: 681). So can the reported marker *dizque* in Colombian Spanish (Alcázar 2018: 730–2) and the reported evidential in Tsou, a Formosan language (Pan 2018: 671). In these three languages the reported evidential with a Noun Phrase scope has the meaning of 'doubt' and can be translated as 'purported' or 'so-called'. The reported evidential with a clausal scope only refers to a speech report and has no such overtones – a minimal pair in Ilonggo is in (59)–(60). In (59), the speaker expresses doubt as to the nature of the debt, hence the translation 'purported'.

(59) Matapus   mabuhin   [ʔaŋ   kunu   ʔutaŋ   niya ...]ₙₚ,   Ilonggo
     after   deducting ABS   REP   debt   3SG.GEN
     naka-kaput   gid   man siya   siŋ   diyutay ŋa kwarta.
     ABIL.REAL-hold   INTENS   ?   3SG.ABS   OBL   little   LK money
     'After deducting her purported debt ..., she was able to keep some money at last'

In (60), the reported evidential *kunu* retains its clausal scope and an evidential meaning of just the information source.

(60) [ʔaŋ   ʔimu   kunu   duha   ka   maŋhud]ₙₚ   Ilonggo
     ABS   2SG.GEN   REP   two   LK   younger.sibling
     didtu   sa   ʔinyu   lula   kag   nagaʔiskwila   man
     there   LOC   2PL.GEN   grandmother   and   go.to.school   also
     'Your two younger siblings, they say, are with your grandmother and are going to school also'

Similarly, the reported evidential *dizque*, literally 'says-that', in various South American Spanishes can have a clause or a noun phrase within its scope. In (38), from Colombian Spanish, its scope is the whole sentence. In (61), the scope of *dizque* is a reason clause introduced with the conjunction *porque* 'because' (Travis 2006: 1276).

(61) nos   dijo   a   Beatriz   *Colombian Spanish*
    1PL.DAT   say.3SG.PRET to   Beatriz
    y   a   mí   que   la   acompañáramos
    and   to   me   CMPL 3SG.ACC   accompany.1PL.SBJ
    al   cementerio   Campos de Paz,
    to.the   cemetery   Campos de Paz
    porque   *dizque*   iba   a   enterrar   a   una   persona
    because   REP   go-3SG.IMPF   to   bury.INF   to   one   person
    'She said to Beatriz and me that we should go with her to the 'Fields of Peace' cemetery, because reportedly (*dizque*) she was going to bury a person'

Dizque can also have a noun phrase within its scope, something Travis (2006: 1287–8) refers to as its 'labelling' function, presenting a label as something the speaker does not fully accept. Such uses are translatable as 'so-called'. The 'labelling' *dizque* with a noun phrase may mark a name the speaker finds unusual, or a name the speaker is unsure of. In (62), the speaker is talking about a type of computer virus called *capa*, but is not certain of the correct name.

(62) tengo   uno   tengo   *Colombian Spanish*
    have.1SG   one   have.1SG
    dizque   el   capa   o algo   así
    REP   ART.DEF   capa   or something   like.that
    'I have got one, I have got *reportedly* (*dizque*) the *capa*, or something like that'

Dizque with the scope over an infinitival complement has an overtone of pretence (see Travis 2006: 1291). A similar example from Mexican Spanish is in (63) (Alcázar 2018: 731, see also Olbertz 2007: 162).[11]

(63) A   los   seis   meses   de   andar   *Mexican Spanish*
    at   ART.PL   six   months   of   go.INFIN
    dizque   gobernando   se   puso   enfermo.
    REP   governing   REFL   got.PRET   sick
    'After having gone about *pretending* (reportedly/*dizque*) to rule for six months he fell ill.'

---

11 See also Pan (2014: 671) and Yang (2000a) on similar semantic differences between an evidential with a clausal scope and with an NP scope in Tsou, a Formosan language.

In contrast, evidentials used with NP scope in Jarawara have the same meaning as those with clausal scope.[12]

The system of non-propositional evidentiality may be radically different from that of evidentiality with a clausal or a sentential scope. In Lakondê, a Nambikwara language, noun phrases distinguish visual proximal and visual distant evidential forms. A four-term evidentiality system with sentential scope is associated with verbs, and involves visual, dual visual, nonvisual and inferred (Eberhard 2018: 344–5) (further examples in Jacques 2018). We return to further correlations between propositional and non-propositional evidentials in section 6.3.

Having non-propositional evidentiality can be considered a relatively rare feature (as it has been attested in fewer than a couple of dozen languages). The ability of having a NP – rather than a clause – within its scope is comparable with the phenomenon of nominal tense and nominal aspect (see Nordlinger and Sadler 2004, Bertinetto 2020, and Aikhenvald 2021b, for an up-to-date approach to non-propositional tense and further references). In a few cases, modal distinctions may have an NP rather than the whole clause in their scope (see Nordlinger and Sadler 2004: 492–3 on 'modal case' in Kayardild; see also Chang 2015 on Tsou, and Nikolaeva 2015 on modal components of nominal tense and aspects in Tundra Nenets, and Lecarme 2008, on Somali). Iatê, a Macro-Jê language from north-eastern Brazil, appears to be able to express potential meanings – which can be interpreted as instances of the 'nominal reality status' – on an NP (see Lapenda 1968: 77–79; Aikhenvald 2015b: 160).

Similarly to some propositional evidentials, evidentials used exclusively with a noun phrase in their scope can have epistemic extensions (see examples (103)–(104) from Maaka, a Chadic language, and Storch and Coly 2014: 196–7, and dubitative overtones of reported evidential *kunu* in Ilonggo in (59) and of *dizque* in (61)–(63)).

An example of intentional modality with a NP within its scope comes from Jarawara (Dixon 2004: 489, 307), *otaa taboro-bonehe-jaa* at our intended dwelling place' in (64).

---

12 There is one formal difference between what Dixon (2004: 306–9) refers to as 'predicate suffixes on noun phrases' (e.g. *-mete-* and *moneha* in (58)) and the same set of tense-modal markers with propositional scope: the initial *-hV-* syllable which is included on tense-modal suffixes in certain contexts never occurs with the same markers on NPs.

(64) otaa   kobo   *Jarawara*
     1EXC.S arrive
     to-witiha-*hamaro*
     AWAY-FROM.PLACE-FAR.PAST.EYEWITNESS.FEM
     otaa-ke   [otaa   taboro-bonehe   jaa]NP
     1EXC-DECL.FEM 1EXC   dwelling.place+MASC-INT.FEM PERI
     'We arrived at what was to be the place where we were to stay'

The option of having a noun phrase within its scope is a feature shared by evidentiality and epistemic modality.

3.2 *Double Marking of Information Source*

Instances of multiple marking of information source in one clause offer the following options, in sections 3.2.1–3.2.3 (see also Aikhenvald 2014: 10–12; 2004: 87–95).

3.2.1 Different Evidentials within One Clause Have Different Scope

This is what we saw in section 3.1.4. For instance, in (58), from Jarawara, the noun phrase is within the scope of a reported evidential, and the sentence itself is cast in the eye-witnessed evidential. The content of the noun phrase is known via a speech report. The actions within the sentence were seen by the speaker.

3.2.2 One Information Source within a Sentence Specifies the Other, with the Same Scope

For instance, in Ersu, a Tibeto-Burman language (Zhang 2014: 142), the inferred evidential can co-occur with either reported or quotative evidential. In (65), the inference – that the person must have been to the town – is based on what the speaker was told by someone else, that is, on a speech report. This is reflected in the order of the evidentials: the inferred evidential always comes before the reported evidential.

(65) thə   ya-ṇo   kuaṣa   *Ersu*
     3SG.PRESENT.SPEAKER   last-day:yesterday   MC:town
     dua-pà~=dzě̌
     go.PAST=EVID:INFERENTIAL=EVID:REPORTED
     'It is said that he must have been to the town yesterday'

Along similar lines, a direct evidential in Lhasa Tibetan can be accompanied by the reported marker, specifying the fact that the speech report comes from someone who has direct information about the statement. This is shown in (66) (Eric Mélac, p.c., taken from his Tibet Student Corpus, and also Mélac 2014: 407, 507).

(66) bu   de   yag.po   'dug=ze   *Lhasa Tibetan*
     boy   DEM   good   DIR.EV=REP
     'He is a good boy' (reported by someone who has information acquired through a direct source = I was told by someone who knows through direct perception or contact with the boy that this boy is good.)

The reported evidential enclitic in both (65) and (66) follows the other evidential specification, iconically reflecting the order in which information source is presented. The reported evidential in both languages is the result of a relatively recent grammaticalization of a speech verb, whose original lexical form is *dʐi* 'say' in Ersu (Zhang 2014: 136) and *zer* 'say' in Lhasa Tibetan (Mélac 2014, 2019, and p.c.). The final position of the reported marker in both languages could be partly explained by its origin, as suggested by Eric Mélac (p.c.).

The source of a speech report may be specified by an additional evidential, and this can be iconically reflected in the order of evidential markers. In Yongning Na (Mosuo), another Tibeto-Burman language, the quotative evidential may co-occur with inferred evidential (Lidz 2007: 67), meaning that the act of speech (and thus the quotation) was inferred (numbers reflect tones).

(67) "ɕi33 gi13   ze33"   *Yongning Na*
     rain   CHANGE.OF.STATE.MARKER
     pi33   *pʰæ33 di33*
     QUOTATIVE   INFERRED
     'It is inferred (that) s/he says, "It's raining"'

The quotation is inferred. This is reflected in the order of evidentials. A similar example involving an inferred and a reported evidential is in (68) (Lidz 2007: 66: the verb 'seem' translates the inferred evidential).

(68) ɕi33 gi13   ze33   pʰæ33 di33   tsi13
     rain   CHANGE.OF.STATE.MARKER   INFERRED   REP
     'It is said that it seems to be raining'

Here, the speech report is based on an inference. The order of evidentials mirrors this.

In (69), the order of evidential markers is the opposite of (68): the reported evidential follows the inferred term. This order iconically reflects the fact that the inference is based on a speech report.

(69) ɕi33 gi13   ze33   tsi13   pʰæ33 di33
     rain   CHANGE.OF.STATE.MARKER   REP   INFERRED
     'It seems that it is said that it's raining'

Both the reported and the quotative evidentials in Yongning Na result from transparent and relatively recent grammaticalization from verbs of speech. The reported evidential *tsi13* has been grammaticalised from the verb *tsi13* 'say', still used as a full lexical verb in the language. The quotative evidential *pi33* is the result of grammaticalization of another speech verb *pi33* 'say, be called' (Lidz 2007: 51–2, 54–5). Neither marker has undergone any phonological depletion in grammaticalization. This suggests the absence of a direct logical link between the degree of grammaticalization of evidentials and their relative position with regard to one another. The principle of iconicity prevails. If a speech report is based on inference, as in (68), the reported evidential follows the inferred. If the inference is based on a speech report, the order is the opposite, as in (69).

Further similar examples have been attested in Tibeto-Burman and Amazonian languages (see Aikhenvald 2014: 11, 2004: 87–95, and Table 3.2 there). Examples (79) and (80) from Matses illustrate the same phenomenon.

3.2.3   Two Co-occurring Evidentials May Mark Two Information Sources, One Additional to the Other

In the instances attested, E(vidential) 1 marks the information source of a character and E(vidential) 2 marks that of the narrator. This is illustrated in (70), from Eastern Pomo (McLendon 2003: 111–112). Here the reported evidential co-occurs with the inferred evidential. The inferred evidential reflects the narrator's inference (and also his lack of certainty, as this evidential does have epistemic overtones). In contrast, the reported indicates that the narrator acquired the story from someone else. This comes from a story about the Bear who killed his daughter-in-law, the Deer.

(70) ka·lél=xa=kʰí   ma·ʔóral   qʼá·-ne-le   Eastern Pomo
     simply=they.say=3pA   daughter.in.law   leave-INFR-REP
     'He must have simply left his daughter-in-law there, they say'

A similar example is in (71). This comes from a description of the part of the comic strip 'Tintin in Tibet' recounted by the speakers to Eric Mélac (p.c.). At this point, the characters of the story hear terrifying shouting from the yeti. The fact that the sentence comes from a story is reflected in the reported evidential. The characters had direct experience of the terrifying noise – and this is reflected in the direct evidential, whose information source comes from the characters.

(71) tsa.bo='i   skad.sgra   cig   *Lhasa Tibetan*
     terrifying=GEN   noise   DEF
     sleb-*song-ze*
     arrive/occur-DIR.EV.AORIST-REP
     'There was a terrifying noise (according to the story)' (that is, the story says that the characters experienced a terrifying noise)

In the majority of instances, only two markers of information source can co-occur within one clause. The only example of three information sources in one clause comes from Tsafiki, a Barbacoan language (Dickinson 2000: 408). The reported marker can be repeated to indicate up to three sources 'between the speaker and the original event'. Each source is connected to the previous one. Two sources are indicated in (72) and three in (73).

(72) tsachi-la   jo-la-jo-*ti*-e   *ti*-e   *Tsafiki*
     person-PL   be-PL-VCL.BE-REP-DECL   say-DECL
     'They say he said they were people'

(73) Man-to=ka   ji-*ti*-e   ti-*ti*-e   *ti*-e
     other-earth=LOC   go-REP-DECL   say-REP-DECL   say-DECL
     'They say that they say that they say that he went to Santo Domingo'

No instances of double marking of egophoricity or mirativity within one clause or sentence have been attested.

Two markers of modality can occur together within one form in highly synthetic languages. In (74), from Kwaza, an isolate from southern Amazonia in Brazil (van der Voort 2004: 412, 606–7), the potential modality (referring to uncertain future) co-occurs with the marker of purposive modality.

(74) ɛ-da-'te-tsy-rjỹ   *Kwaza*
     go-1S–PURP-POT-NOM.CD:area
     'the place where she was going to/prepared to go (together) to'

In a few instances across the world, two markers of epistemic modalities can occur in one clause. A marker of uncertainty can occur together with a marker of counterexpectation in Tariana (Aikhenvald 2003a: 387–90). In Alto Perené (Mihas 2015: 229) optative and dubitative modal markers can co-occur. Two modal meanings can occur together in some varieties of English, e.g. dialectal *He might could go*. Similarly to the ways in which evidentials can occur together – described under 3.2.2 – the co-occurring epistemic modals reflect different facets of the attitudes of the same person. There are no analogies in the domain of epistemic modality to different evidentials reflecting different perceivers of information or its 'reporters' (as in (70)–(73) above). In other words, there are no instances of co-occurring epistemic modality markers reflecting the attitude of different characters, or speakers.

We conclude that having more than one exponent reflecting different information sources, especially those coming from different participants, is a specific feature of evidentials, only partially shared with epistemic modalities.

3.3 *Independent Time Reference of Evidentials*

An evidential can have its own time reference, different from that of the clause or the sentence. In this way, evidentials are different from other categories: an epistemic modal or an egophoric or a mirative marker will never have their own time reference (see discussion in Aikhenvald 2004: 99–102, 2014: 10–12; 2015a: 261).

In Tariana, the reported evidential marks the time of the speech report (not that of the event). In (75), the speaker had just been told that information would happen in the future. The future marker refers to the timing of the event: her coming in the future. The recent past reported evidential reflects the timing of the speech report.

(75) du-nu-karu-*pidaka* *Tariana*
3sgnf-come-PURPOSIVE-REC.P.REPORTED
'She will return reportedly' (the speaker has been told recently)

If the speaker had been told a long time ago about a future event, they would use the remote past reported evidential:

(76) du-nu-karu-*pidana* *Tariana*
3sgnf-come-PURPOSIVE-REM.P.REPORTED
'She will return reportedly' (the speaker was told a long time ago)

Similar examples are found in Tucano.

The tense forms of evidentials in Tariana and in the neighbouring East Tukanoan languages of the Vaupés River Basin contain reference to the time of acquisition of information, and whether the information is still accessible

(Aikhenvald 2003a: 289, 2004: 100–2, Ramirez 1997: 125–6, Stenzel and Gomez-Imbert 2018: 378–9). A Tariana speaker was asked if he had the key to the house. He answered (77): he had seen the key some time ago (but could not see it now).

(77) alia-*na*　　　　　　　　　　　　　　　　　　　　　　　*Tariana*
 exist-REM.P.VIS
 'It was (with me)' (I saw it previously)

A similar example is in (78), from Tukano, the major lingua franca of the Brazilian of the Vaupés River Basin Linguistic area. Here, the speaker saw Pedro at school a few minutes before the moment of speech. A literal translation could be '(I saw in the recent past) (Pedro) being at school' (Ramirez 1997: 125–6).

(78) bu'ê-dó-pɨ　　　　　　　　　　dɨ̃-abɨ̃　　　　　　　　*Tukano*
 study-LOCATIVE.NOMINALISATION-FOC　be-REC.P.VIS
 '(Pedro) is/was at school (I saw him a few minutes ago)'

This is consistent with the ways in which the reported evidentials in (75) and (76) have reference to the timing of a speech report rather than the event. Along similar lines, a special evidential marker which marks remembered events in Turkish reflects the timing of the information source – that is, the past experience one recalls (Johanson and Csató ms).

The time of speaker's acquisition of information may be fused with an evidential. Kalmyk, a Mongolic language, has several inferred evidentials whose choice depends on whether the inference was made based on what happened at the moment of speech, or before it (Skribnik and Seesing 2014: 153; Brosig and Skribnik 2018: 567). Foe, a Kutubuan language (Sarvasy 2018: 646–7) has an inferred evidential based on previously visible results, and an inferred evidential based on results which are currently visible. Perceptual evidentials in Korean (Sohn 2018) contrast 'prior perception' (the marker *-te*) and 'instantaneous perception' (the marker *-ney*). The 'prior perception' (or 'retrospective') evidential has the semantic feature of 'past time' of speaker's perception.

In Kaluli, a Bosavi language from New Guinea, a reported evidential has different forms depending on when the speaker received the information (Sarvasy 2018: 640; Grosh and Grosh 2004: 27–8). The 'past reported action' form will be used if the information was acquired some time ago. If the reported information was acquired only recently, one opts for the present reported form. 'Reported past' and 'reported future' evidential markers are distinguished in Kamula, an isolate of the Western Province in Papua New Guinea: Sarvasy 2018: 634–5; Routamaa 1994: 26–27, 29–30).

Alternatively, two information sources, each with its own time reference, can be marked on one predicate within a sentence. This has been described for Matses, a Panoan language (Fleck 2007). Evidentiality in Matses has sentential scope (no evidential distinctions are made within dependent clauses, and there is no non-propositional evidentiality).

A hunter will say (79), if he SAW fresh tracks of a white-lipped peccary a short time ago. The experiential evidential reflects the fact that he saw the tracks. The inferred evidential shows that the tracks are the basis for inference that the peccary has been here:

(79) Şhëktenamë   *Matses*
     white.lipped.peccary
     kuen-*ak-o*-şh
     pass.by-REC.PAST.INFERRED-REC.PAST.EXPERIENTIAL-3p
     'White-lipped peccaries evidently passed by (here)' (fresh tracks were discovered a short time ago)

If the hunter HAD SEEN the tracks of a white-lipped peccary a long time ago, and the tracks were fresh, he will use distant past experiential, and recent past inferred: the inference relates to the fact that the peccaries have been here recently, with respect to some time long ago when he had discovered them:

(80) Şhëktenamë   *Matses*
     white.lipped.peccary
     kuen-*ak-onda*-şh
     pass.by-REC.PAST.INFERRED-DISTANT.PAST.EXPERIENTIAL-3p
     'White-lipped peccaries evidently passed by (here)' (fresh tracks were discovered a long time ago)

There is no evidence that any of the evidentials in Matses or other Panoan languages had originated in independent verbs (see Valenzuela 2003: 52–7; Fleck 2007). Instances of independent time marking in evidentials appear to be cross-linguistically rare. This may be due to the lack of detailed analytic grammars of languages with evidentiality.

3.4   *Ability to Be Negated Independently from the Predicate*

An evidential can be within the scope of negation (Hansson 1994: 6, 2003; see also Egerod 1985, and the discussion in Aikhenvald 2004: 256–7). In (81), from Akha, a Tibeto-Burman language, the visual information source and not the verb itself is being negated (Hansson 2003: 249).

(81) àjɔ̃~q   áŋ   dì   ə   *Akha*
     he   NOUN.PARTICLE   beat   VERB.PARTICLE
     àshú ɣà   mà   ŋá
     who   not   VIS
     'I do not know/can't see who is beating him'

The ability of being negated separately from the predicate sets evidentiality apart from other categories related to knowledge. So far, Akha appears to offer the only example of this phenomenon.

3.5   *Ability to Be Questioned Separately from the Predicate*

In many languages, when a question is formed on a clause marked for evidentiality, the action or state may be questioned, rather than the information source. However, in some systems, the information source (that is, the evidential) can be questioned. Consider the following dialogue, from Wanka Quechua (Floyd 1999: 132). In (83), M. queries the source of information R. has in (82), and the appropriateness of the reported evidential.

(82) R.   wasi-i-ta   am-*shi*   yayku-llaa-la-nki   *Wanka Quechua*
          house-1p-ACC   you-REP   enter-LIM-PAST-2p
          'They say you entered my house'

(83) M.   mayan-taa   ni-n
          who-SCORN   say-3p
          'WHO says that?!'

   R. answers, referring to a different information source:

(84) R.   nuna   lika-a-niki   ka-ña   achka-*m*   *Wanka Quechua*
          person   see-AG-2p   be-NONPAST   much-DIR.EV
          'There are lots of people who saw you'

A similar example from Japanese is in (85) (Narrog and Yang 2018: 719).

(85) Ooshima   Yuuko=mo   *Japanese*
      PN   PN=FOC
      iNtai~s.uru=*soo*=des.u=ka?
      retire~do.NONPAST=EVID=COP.NPAST=INTER
      'Is it being said that Yuko Oshima also retires?' (www.ztcizpnqixeh.
      exwweragi.xyz/)

As Narrog and Yang (2018: 720) put it, with *soo* in (85) 'it is apparently the reporting as such, which unlike in the case of the reportative *rasi-* is independent of speaker judgment (cf. section 2), that is questioned.' (They also seem to imply that this evidential can also be within the scope of negation; but no examples are given).

A speaker can doubt or query the use of an evidential. In Bora, as Thiesen and Weber (2012: 306) put it, 'if a speaker fails to include an evidential clitic when reporting an event he or she did not witness, they may be challenged by the hearer' (Wojtylak 2018). Eric Mélac (p.c.) reports how he had commented on the conditions in Chinese prisons, using a visual evidential. His interlocutor expressed surprise – the use of visual evidential implied that Eric had himself been inside a Chinese prison (which was not the case).

The wrong use of evidential may be corrected if the interlocutor knows that the information source was wrong. There are numerous fieldwork-based examples to this effect.

Bob Dixon recounts how one morning he had come out of his hut in the Jarawara village and noticed that a tree, *awa*, had fallen (*-sona-*) while he had been asleep. He immediately said (86), using the witnessed form:

(86) Awa   sona-*hara*-ke   *Jarawara*
     tree   fall-IMM.PAST.EYEWITNESS.FEM-DECL.FEM
     'The tree has fallen over' (eyewitness)

This was at once corrected by Motobi, a speaker of Jarawara who happened to be around. Although Bob did see that the tree had fallen, he did not actually see it toppling over: using *-harake* would have implied exactly that. So his Jarawara teacher suggested (87), the appropriate way of phrasing the information source available to Bob at that point (Dixon 2016: 90).

(87) Awa   sona-*hani*-ke   *Jarawara*
     tree   fall-IMM.PAST.NONEYEWITNESS.FEM-DECL.FEM
     'The tree has fallen over' (noneyewitness: I didn't see it happen)

Speakers of languages with evidentials are prepared to discuss why a particular evidential had been used, and query the wrong or unwarranted uses of evidentials. In Tariana, dreams by common mortals are cast in nonvisual evidentials. Only shamans and people with supranatural powers have prophetic dreams. Their account is cast in visual evidential. In (88), a shaman sees his grandfather in a dream and says upon waking up:

(88) wa-hweri-ne   ikasu-nuku   *Tariana*
    1pl-grandfather-FOC.A/S now-TOP.NON.A/S
    ma:tsi-pu-*naka*   diha
    bad-AUG-PRES.VIS   he
    'Right now our grandfather is in a bad way' – VISUAL

The rest of the story confirms that he was right: an evil spirit had come and devoured the grandfather. When I asked Jovino Brito to confirm that I had understood the evidential correctly, he replied (89).

(89) mariẽri-pu-*na*   di-ka-*na*   thui-niki   *Tariana*
    shaman-AUG-REM.P.VIS   3sgnf-see-PRES.VIS   all-COMPL
    'He is a real shaman (lit. very much a shaman, or big shaman), he has been seeing everything'

'Lexical reinforcement' of evidential markers further confirms speakers' metalinguistic awareness of information source in grammar. If a speaker uses a particular evidential, they may choose to strengthen the source by adding a lexical explanation. Frequently, if a speaker did see something and tells a story about it in visual evidential; but then realizes that their audience may be a bit incredulous, they may choose to strengthen his 'visual source' by saying 'I saw it'. In (90), the storyteller used the remote past visual evidential to stress that he had himself seen the stone – one of the traces left by the Creator of Manioc – which is still there. The rest of the story is told in remote past reported. This lexical 'reinforcement' provides additional evidence in favour of 'seeing' as the basic semantics for the visual evidential.

(90) di-ruku-i-ta-ka   diha kainiki-da   *Tariana*
    3sgnf-go.down-CAUS1-CAUS2-SUB ART   manioc-CL:ROUND
    di-wha-*na*   nu-ka-*na*   nuha
    3sgnf-stay-REM.P.VIS   1sg-see-REM.P.VIS   I
    kasina-misini   diha-da-nuku
    now-TOO   ART-CL:ROUND-TOP.NON.A/S
    'Downstream from it (a rapid) there is the manioc stone, I have seen it, too.'

A story about the 'good olden days' told by the late Américo Brito, the oldest living speaker of Tariana I ever met, raised a few eyebrows – the audience looked incredulously as he was expostulating about how great life was in the days of his childhood, before missionaries took charge. He then chose to stress that had seen it all with his own eyes, emphatically repeating 'I saw it, I saw it when I was a child', to make his statement sound even stronger, in (91).

(91) hiku-*na* na-ni na-yã-*na,* nu-kesi-do, *Tariana*
thus-REM.P.VIS 3pl-do 3pl-live-REM.P.VIS 1sg-relative-FEM
pedale-pe-se, nhua-niri-pe-se nha kayu
old-PL-CONTR 1sg+parent-MASC-PL-CONTR they like.this
na-ni-ka, nu-ka-*na,* nhua yanape-ka nu-ka-*na*
3pl-do-SUB 1sg-see-REM.P.VIS I child-SUB 1sg-see-REM.P.VIS
mẽda
COUNTEREXP
'This is how they lived, my relative, old people, our parents (not anyone else), I saw them do thus, when I was a child I did see them.'

Metalinguistic comments by speakers show their awareness of why a particular evidential has to be used. This awareness reflects the way in which evidentials are embedded in the social environment and people's perception of it (see also Aikhenvald 2004: 360, and section 3.6).

There are no examples of modality, egophoricity, or mirativity within the scope of a question, in the same way as evidentials. Whether or not speakers or language learners get corrected when they use erroneous or unsubstantiated marking of access to information (egophoricity), attitude to information (epistemic modality), or expectation of knowledge (mirativity) remains a moot point. Metalinguistic awareness of evidentials sets them apart from other grammatical categories, including mirativity, epistemic modality, and perhaps also egophoricity.

3.6 *Correlations with Speech Genres and Social Environment*

What further distinguishes evidentials from other grammatical means used to express knowledge is their embeddedness in cultural practices and attitudes to the ways in which knowledge is framed. Reported evidential is often used as a token of story genre. For instance, stories transmitted throughout generations will be cast in reported or an assumed evidential (see examples in Aikhenvald 2004, 2014, 2018a, and references there; and also section 4.3).

An established evidential can be associated with a particular type of experience. In a number of languages, including Tariana, Tucano, and the traditional Wintu (as described by Lee 1938), the nonvisual evidential is used for supernatural phenomena and shamanic experience (similar examples, from Tariana, are in (114)–(116)). The Trio and the Wayana, speakers of Carib languages with just two evidentials, witnessed and unwitnessed, describe shamanic attacks using the unwitnessed form (Carlin 2018). The nonvisual evidential marker ŋa- in Dyirbal was used when talking about spirits (Dixon 2014: 186–7). The 'auditive' evidential in Nenets (a Samoyedic language) is used when talking about shamanic activities (Ilyina 2017: 167–9). Preferences in the use of evidentials across different discourse genres are restricted by conventional representation of information source available for different experiences (along the lines of Wood 2018: 251–6). Depending on their status in the community, a speaker will be entitled to recounting stories associated with specific evidential choices – we return to this in section 4.3.

The use of evidentials tends to mirror changes in social environment. The introduction of new technologies warrants new uses of evidentials. Among the Tariana, information via television, internet, and mobile phone are now considered tantamount to what one sees or face-to-face interaction. Information via short-wave radio is treated as 'nonvisual'. Speakers of Hinuq and of Tatar use the non-witnessed form for what they had seen on TV or heard on the radio. In contrast, the Na of Luoshui use the direct, or firsthand, evidential to relate what they had seen on television. If one hears the information on television but cannot see the picture, the reported evidential is used (Lidz 2007: 67). For the Shipibo-Konibo, watching something on television is tantamount to information acquired directly (using the firsthand evidential -ra). The information heard on the radio and over the phone is marked as reported (using the reported evidential -ronki). The same evidential is used for the information obtained by reading, including internet, newspapers and books. A Shipibo-Konibo teacher commented that 'if one reads in a book about the location of a given place, -ronki would be used' – an example is in (92).

(92) Alemania-*ronki*   Holanda   patax   iki   *Shipibo-Konibo*
     Germany-REP   The.Netherlands next.to COP
     'Germany is next to The Netherlands' (reported information: I read it in a book)

'If one obtains the same information from a map, -ra would be appropriate instead' (Valenzuela 2003: 52–3). This is what we see in (93).

(93) Alemania-*ra*   Holanda   patax   iki   *Shipibo-Konibo*
     Germany-DIR.EV   The.Netherlands next.to COP
     'Germany is next to The Netherlands' (direct evidential: I saw it on a map)

The Tariana of northwest Amazonia treat communication via social media and WhatsApp as tantamount to face-to-face conversations, using the visual evidential (see more on such changes in Aikhenvald 2014: 35, 2018a: 28–9).

In contrast, we have no evidence as to whether modality, egophoricity, and mirativity ever adjust to new practices of acquisition and processing of knowledge. In all likelihood, they do not, as their use is much less culture- and practice-bound than that of evidentials.

Evidentials are tokens of the integration of language and society (along the lines of Aikhenvald, Dixon, and Jarkey 2021). Obligatory use of evidentials correlates with the requirement to be precise in one's information source, and in being careful about what is said. Within the north-west Amazonian context, this is related to a common belief that there is an explicit cause for everything, especially for adverse events. So as not to attract suspicions of having secret powers or knowledge, one needs to be careful in always saying how one knows things. 'White people's' language (Portuguese or Spanish) does not have to mark information source. Many Indians comment that White people are not to be trusted because they never tell you how they know things. They are thus suspected of having something to hide or perhaps of having some hidden malicious powers. Lexical expression of information source has grown to be a feature of the local variety of Portuguese spoken by most indigenous people within the Vaupés River Basin area: 'I saw' for 'visual', 'I didn't see' for nonvisual, 'I have proof' for inferred based on visual traces, 'it appears' for assumed, and 'it is said that' for the reported (expressed with *dizque*, literally, 'says-that', a wide-spread feature of Amazonian Portuguese and Spanish on the whole: see Alcázar 2018, Aikhenvald 2020). More on this in section 5.

In many Amazonian societies, clear and precise expression defines a person's 'worth'. Among the Mamaindê, a Northern Nambikwara group from southern Amazonia, a typical way of referring to a 'good, trustworthy person' is to invoke their capacity to use the language properly, and employ evidentials in an appropriate manner. Someone who is 'untrustworthy or of a questionable moral reputation is labelled as one who does not speak well' (Eberhard 2009: 468). The correct use of evidentials is a special 'token' of a good speaker and henceforth, a good, reliable, and trustworthy person.

The same principle applies to the Tariana (and also the East Tukanoan peoples in the Vaupés River Basin area: see Aikhenvald 2013, 2015a: 267–76). Those who use the wrong evidentials are called *mẽda-peni* 'those good for nothing, useless' in Tariana. The same term applies to those who do not know traditional lore and are hapless in other ways.

The ways in which evidentials are embedded in cultural practices and beliefs may account for their 'aggressive' spread from one language to the next when languages are in contact. Shared discourse genres, speech practices and attitudes to information underlie their propensity for areal diffusion (more on this in Aikhenvald 2018b). As Storch (2018: 617) put it, 'the sociolinguistic history of the African settings where evidential marking is a common feature in a variety of unrelated languages suggests that there are particular contact settings that are likely to enhance the emergence of evidential marking', among them heteroglossic practices (characteristic of numerous languages with evidentials, including Hone, a Jukunoid language). At present, we have no such evidence for diffusibility of egophoricity, mirativity, or epistemic modality.

3.7 *How Evidentials Are Special: Interim Conclusions*

As shown in Table 3, evidentials stand apart from other categories related to knowledge with regard to the following properties.

First, evidentiality can have variable scope. This is a feature shared with epistemic modality, but not with egophoricity or mirativity.

Secondly, more than one information source can be marked within one clause (resulting in co-occurrence of evidentials within a clause. This feature is partially shared with epistemic modality, but not with egophoricity or mirativity.

Thirdly, an evidential may have its own time reference. This feature is unique to evidentiality.

Fourthly, an evidential can be negated or questioned without negating or questioning the propositional content. This feature is unique to evidentiality.

The use of evidentials reflects cultural practices and attitudes. Evidentials tend to be sensitive to societal changes, adapting to new ways of obtaining information (including television, phone, and social media). Different speech genres can be characterised by special evidentials as tokens of genres. These features set evidentiality apart from all other categories related to knowledge.

In Hill and Irvine's (1992: 17) words, 'knowledge is a social phenomenon, an aspect of the social relations between people'. Evidentials are a testimony to this – more than any other knowledge-related category. The special status of evidentiality, with the source of knowledge as its primary meaning, is reflected in its sensitivity to different kinds of experiences and to social change. Describing a language with evidentials without taking account of the society and the attitudes of the speakers would result in a bleached and colourless account – an emaciated skeleton of a language rather than a rich body full of life.

This is how Storch (2018: 628) put it: 'the creativity and dynamics that characterise these ways of indicating source of information and of being precise reach beyond language as structure, and tell us something about social and cultural practices'.

4 Access to Information and Information Source: Evidentiality Meets Egophoricity

An evidential term within a closed grammatical system may be semantically complex. The use of an evidential may correlate with access to knowledge. It will then extend into the domain covered by exponents of egophoricity in other languages.

Expressions of physical and mental states are a prime example. Here, the expression of information source typically correlates with privileged access to information by the speaker. This is what we saw in section 2.1, and examples (17)–(20), in section 2. The egophoric overtones of evidentials are typically restricted to one semantic class of verbs and expressions – those to do with internal states and feelings (called 'endophoric' in the Tibeto-Burmanist literature: see, for instance, Sun 2018).

Our focus here is on access to information source within the system of evidentials, not restricted to any type of predicate. The ways of expressing 'general' or 'common' knowledge – not limited to any specific class of experience – are a case in point.

Languages with a special term reflecting 'general knowledge' are the topic of section 4.1. An evidential term can combine information source with reference to access to information and information sharing – the topic of section 4.2. Alternatively, an evidential may have an additional meaning of communally shared knowledge: we turn to this in section 4.3.

4.1 *'General Knowledge': A Term in an Evidentiality System*

A special form for general, or 'common', knowledge is a feature of a few multi-term systems with at least three other evidential terms.

Yongning Na (Mosuo), a Tibeto-Burman language (Lidz 2007), has a direct or visual, inferential, reported and quotative evidential. Some evidentials can occur together, as shown in (67)–(69). A further term covers general knowledge. This marker is illustrated in (94) (Lidz 2007: 61; we can recall that numbers represent tones).

(94) na13   bu33   na13   bu33   *Yongning Na*
     Na   POSS   Na   POSS
     zɨ33 tu33-kuɔ33   dɨ31 ta13   tɔ31
     family-LOC   all   COMPARATIVE
     tsA33=dʐO33
     important/busy=COMMON.KNOWLEDGE.EVID
     zɨ33   mi33   tʰɨ33   li33   ni31
     hearth   room   this   CL   COP
     'In Na families, more important than anything, as everyone knows, is the hearth room'

The common knowledge evidential can occur together with each of the reported, the inferred, and the quotative evidential. In (95), a statement of 'common knowledge' is based on a speech report (Lidz 2007: 65).

(95) na13   bu33   na13   bu33   zɨ33 tu33-kuɔ33   *Yongning Na*
     Na   POSS   Na   POSS   family-LOC
     dɨ31   ta13   tɔ31   tsa33=dʐɔ33
     all   COMPARATIVE   important/busy=COMMON.KNOWLEDGE.EVID
     zɨ33   mi33   tʰɨ33   li33   ni31
     hearth   room   this   CL   COP
     tsi13
     REP
     'It is said, in Na families, more important than anything, as everyone knows, is the hearth room'

The common knowledge evidential in Yongning Na 'receives epistemic readings of a good degree of certainty, as it indicates that something is generally accepted as being true' (Lidz 2007: 60). Generally, its scope is a sentence; but it can extend to more than that, as it can be 'pragmatically available for several sentences' (in contrast to other evidentials in the language).

Kalmyk (Skribnik and Seesing 2014: 163; Brosig and Skribnik 2018: 568–9) also has a special evidential for 'common knowledge'. An evidential construction *-dg ginä* (habitual participle in *-d(g)* + grammaticalised form of the quotation verb *gi-*) occurs mainly in proverbs, referring to what everyone one knows (along the lines of Lidz 2007: 60–63). In (96), the participial construction which literally translates as 'having become-said', marks what everyone knows. The construction is in brackets.

(96) äämtx-äg   asr-ž   tus   uga   *Kalmyk*
    coward-ACC   care-CONVB.IMPF   use   NEG
    [bol-*d-mn*   *ginä*]
    become-PARTIC.HAB-AFF   'SAY'.GRAMMATICALISED
    'Taking care of a coward is useless (as everyone knows)'

In Buryat, another Mongolic language (Brosig and Skribnik 2018: 573), 'the quotative verb *ge-* takes direct and indirect speech report complements and is the most important means for expressing reported and quoted information'. Its present tense sociative form (*ge-lse-ne*) grammaticalised specifically for this reportative function. The habitual participle *ge-lse-deg* is used to express common or general knowledge – as shown in (97).

(97) Erdeni   ele-xe   bür'-ee   ünge   *Buryat*
    jewel   wear_out-PARTIC.FUT   POSTP-REFL   colour
    oro-xo   *ge-lse-deg*
    enter-PARTIC.FUT[3SG/PL]   SAY-SOC-PARTIC.HAB
    'The more a jewel wears out, the brighter it gets, as they say'

General knowledge, or common wisdom, is represented through a grammaticalised speech report. This is unlike Yongning Na, where the general or common knowledge evidential is not etymologically linked to any other information source marker.

A special term with the system of evidentials expresses 'general knowledge' in Mamaindê and Southern Nambikwara (both from the Nambikwara family: Eberhard 2018: 337–41, 348–50, 353–6). The evidential refers to 'knowledge that is known (or available to be known) by the whole community as part of the habitual experience of a collective, or part of the body of knowledge that has been passed down from one generation to the next, such as the extensive Nambikwaran mythology' (Eberhard 2018: 339).

Mamaindê adds to this a visual, a nonvisual, an inferred evidential, plus two reported markers: one expressing secondhand information, and the other one expressing thirdhand information. Visual, nonvisual, inferred, and secondhand reported evidential distinguish four tense forms (present, recent past, intermediate past, and distant past). The general knowledge and the thirdhand reported evidentials do not distinguish tenses (we return to this in section 6.1). The system of evidentials and tenses in Mamaindê is in Table 4 (Eberhard 2018: 349; 2012: 141).

TABLE 4   The Mamaindê tense/evidential system

Evidential	Present	Recent past	Intermediate past	Distant past
1. Visual	(-*latʰa* -: only 3rd person)	-nãn	let-nãn	-hĩnʔ
2. Nonvisual	-nha / nhaʔ	-hĩn	-le-hĩn	-le-hĩn
3. Inferred	-sihna	-ntĩn	-le-ntĩn	-sihĩnʔ
4. Reported (2nd hand)	-satau-nha	-satau-hĩn	-satau-le-hĩn	-satau-le-hĩn
5. Reported (3rd hand)		-sĩn-nha		
6. General Knowledge		nĩnta / -ĩnta /-nta		

The following examples illustrate the general knowledge evidential in Mamaindê. The information is known to the whole community because this occurs time and time again, as in (98).

(98) ta-tukwinʔni-tu   ʔaik-tu   *Mamaindê*
    POSS1-father.in.law-FNS   field-FNS
    tau-Ø-nta-wa
    chop-S3-EVID:GEN.KNOW-DECL
    'My father-in-law is clearing a field' (everyone knows this because he's been doing this every day now for a month)

Generally known information may be part of the people's mythological lore – this is the most common usage of the corresponding evidential in Mamaindê.

(99) jahon   ʔaik-tu   tanik-taʔ   *Mamaindê*
    old.man   field-FN   bury-CONJ.AND
    nãn-jeʔ-Ø-*nĩnta*-wa
    cry-EMPH-S3-EVID.GEN.KNOW-DECL
    'They buried the old man in the field and cried' (everyone knows this because it's part of our mythology)

In Southern Nambikwara, the 'general knowledge' evidential is part of a large system which consists of visual, inferred, and reported. For each of these, there is a further distinction between individual knowledge by the speaker and 'dual' knowledge by speaker and addressee (within three tenses). The distinction between 'individual' and dual, or 'shared', knowledge is neutralised in the form expressing general knowledge. The general knowledge evidential does not distinguish tense forms (see also section 6.1). The evidential system in Southern Nambikwara is in Table 5 (Eberhard 2018: 340).

The general knowledge evidential in Southern Nambikwara refers to habitual activities (hence the term 'customary' used in an earlier description by Kroeker 2001). An example is in (100) (Eberhard 2018: 341–2).

(100) ti³ka³l-a²   kai³l-a²   *Southern Nambikwara*
       anteater-DEF   ant-DEF
       yain³-Ø-te²ju²hẽ³-la²
       eat-3SG-EVID:GEN.KNOW/PAST-PERF
       'The anteater habitually eats ants'

The general knowledge evidential is used in myths (Eberhard 2018: 353–5, based on Kroeker p.c.). And it has 'an air of distant past about it, recalling knowledge that was passed down from one generation to the next for centuries, representing the accumulated learning of an entire people. It is that body of historical information that every normal adult in the community is expected to know' (pp. 353–4). This is why 'past' is included in the gloss in (100).

TABLE 5   The Southern Nambikwara dual-paradigm evidential system

	Individual perspective	Dual perspective
Visual		
Present	-na³/(-Ø)	-ti²tu³
Recent Past	-na²/(-Ø)	-te¹ni²tu³/ten¹tu³
Past	-hẽ³/(-na²hẽ³)	-tai¹ti²tu³/tait¹tu³
Inferred		
Present	-nĩn²ta²	-tu¹ti²tu³
Recent Past	-nĩn²su²	-te³nu¹ti²tu³
Past	(-nũ²hẽ³)	-te³nait¹ti²tu³
Reported		
Recent Past	-ta¹hẽ²	-ta¹te¹ti²tu³
Past	-ta¹hẽ¹	-ta¹tẽx¹ti²tu³
Remote Past	-ta¹hxai²hẽ¹	----------------------
General knowledge	-te²ju²hẽ³	

The general knowledge evidential in Mamaindê has epistemic overtones of reliability and trustworthiness. This is in contrast to both reported evidentials which have overtones of doubt (Eberhard 2018: 349, 353). No such overtones have been noted for Southern Nambikwara or other languages with a special form for 'general knowledge'.

There could be more instances of an evidential expressing 'general knowledge'. The clitic =ʔma 'general knowledge' appears to have existed in Central Pomo (now highly obsolescent), alongside visual, nonvisual auditory, reported, and inferential evidential. A statement accompanied with the marker refers to an 'established fact' (Mithun 1999: 181).[13]

General knowledge, or shared knowledge, can be expressed with means other than evidentials. In Munya (Bai 2019: 321), an interrogative tag ɛ-ti (INTER-stative) at the end of a full clause serves to 'elicit confirmation from the addressee and seek rapport between interlocutors'. Ingush has special construction *my Verb=ii* (EMPHATIC verb.PAST=QUESTION), which 'has the form of a question, but is not literally a question. It is used to indicate that something is common knowledge and often to gain the hearer's agreement that it is common knowledge' (Nichols 2011: 723). The connection between expressing common knowledge and interrogative form is reminiscent of what we find in Yongning Na (Lidz 2007: 60): there, the common knowledge evidential comes from transparent grammaticalization of a question marker =aɜ1 followed by the locative/existential verb also used as a progressive marker dzɔ33. The link between interrogatives and information sharing is likely to be due to the interactive nature of questions, which presuppose participation of the audience, or the addressees. A general investigation of how common and shared knowledge is expressed through grammar by means other than evidentials is a matter for a separate cross-linguistic study.

4.2 *Access to Information Source and Knowledge Sharing in Evidentials*

Information sharing, and addressee's access to information may be part of the meaning of an evidential. This can be a feature of just one evidential term. An instance of such a propositional reported evidential is addressed in I. A non-propositional visual evidential is addressed in II.

---

13   In the absence of a full grammar of the language, it is hard to appreciate the exact range of meanings of this, and of other evidentials in the language (see also Bergqvist 2017: 3). McLendon (2003: 124–5) describes the system of seven evidentials in Central Pomo (in the context of other Pomoan languages). Some of them appear to reflect speaker's access to information and thus be potentially considered exponents of egophoricity (cf. Oswalt 1986, on Kashaya).

Alternatively, information sharing can acquire autonomous realization within a number of evidential terms – as shown in III.

I. Access to information and knowledge sharing are distinguished within reported evidentials in Southern Tepehuan (or O'dam), a Uto-Aztecan language. The language has a direct evidential, an inferential evidential, and two evidentials marking reported information. Of these, the evidential -*sap* marks reported information which is not known to the addressee (García Salido 2014a: 25–6), and may have overtones of unreliability (see García Salido 2014b: 98). An example is in (101), where *sap* is glossed as a 'reported evidential referring to unknown information'. The information was not known to the listener (in this case, the researcher herself).

(101) Piam *sap*   ba-tañxi-dha'-am   *Southern Tepehuan*
      DISJ REP.UI COMPL-ask-APPL-3pl.SUBJ
      ma'n   gu   ubii
      one   DET   woman
      'Or they say, they ask for a woman (for him)' (reported unknown to listener)

The evidential -*sak* marks reported information which is either already known to the addressee, or reflects experience shared with the addressee (García Salido 2014a: 28–9). An example is in (102). The speaker recalls 'how it was living with her husband', who was present during the recording; the listener already knew some of the information she was sharing (García Salido 2014b: 102). In (102), the evidential is glossed as referring to reported evidential with known information.

(102) ja-ma-mit   ba'   *sak*   *Southern Tepehuan*
      3pl.PO-give-3pl.SUBJ.PERF SEQ   REP.KI
      gu   despesa   na   mi'   jai'ch-ka-t
      DET   pantry/supplies   SUB   DIRN   exist-EST-IMPF
      'They gave them the supplies that were there' (reported partly known to listener)

This evidential has no epistemic overtones.

II. Access to information and knowledge sharing are distinguished within the visual markers of non-propositional evidentiality in Maaka (Storch and Coly 2014: 196–8). The language has three non-propositional evidentials – visual (perceived by the speaker), joint perception (by speaker and addressee), and assumption. There is only one, reported, evidential with propositional scope. In contrast to other evidentials, the reported term also has epistemic overtones of unreliability and doubt.

The evidential *-dìyà* marking joint perception – with a noun phrase in its scope – is illustrated in (103). Both the speaker and the addressee can see the child.

(103) làa   nàmáa-*dìyà*   sáy   mìnè-pódǐ-ní   *Maaka*
       child this-JOINT:VIS   must   1pl-remove:TEL-OBJ:3sg:MASC
       gè-gòrkù-wà
       LOC-village-DEF
       'This child [whom we can both see], we must chase him from the village'

This is in contrast to the other visual evidential *-mú* which marks something only the speaker, and not the addressee, has seen.

(104) móy   pə̀rpə́r   ním   mákkà-*mú*   *Maaka*
       see.IMP   butterfly REL   Mecca-INDIVIDUAL.VIS
       'See the butterfly from Mecca!' (seen only by the speaker)

The marker of joint perception has additional epistemic overtones of reliability; so does the visual evidential.

III. Access to information source can be expressed within several terms in a multi-term evidential system. As mentioned in section 4.1 and Table 5, Southern Nambikwara distinguishes between individual knowledge by the speaker and 'dual' knowledge by speaker and addressee for each of visual, inferred, and reported evidentials. The distinction between 'individual' and dual, or 'shared', knowledge is neutralised in the form expressing general knowledge (see Eberhard 2018: 340–1; Kroeker 2001, and also Lowe 1999: 276).

In (105), the visual information comes from the speaker: the speaker was the only one to have seen the event. This is reflected in the choice of the 'speaker-only' evidential. Numbers reflect tones.

(105) wa^{3}ko^{3}n-a^1-hẽ^3-la^2 *Southern Nambikwara*
       work-1SG-EVID:VIS.INDV/PAST-PERF
       'I worked yesterday'

In (106), both speaker and addressee saw the event happen, and the corresponding 'dual information source' evidential is used.

(106) wa³ko³n-a¹-*tai¹ti²tu³*-wa² Southern Nambikwara
       work-1SG-EVID:VIS.DUAL/PAST-IMPF
       'You and I saw that I worked'

In (107), only the speaker had access to reported information.

(107) wa³ko³n-Ø-*ta¹hxai²hẽ¹*-la² Southern Nambikwara
       work-3SG-EVID:REP.INDV/REM.PAST-PERF
       'I was told that he worked (in the remote past)'

And in (108), both speaker and addressee know what they are talking about, based on a speech report.

(108) wa³ko³n-Ø-*ta¹tẽx¹ti²tu³*-wa² Southern Nambikwara
       work-3SG-EVID:REP.DUAL/PAST-IMPF
       'We were told that he worked'

The general knowledge evidential reflects information available to everyone, as communal and traditional knowledge. It marks the information between what is available to the speaker and what is available to the addressee. An example is in (100).

In Lakondê, also from the Nambikwara family, only the visual evidential distinguishes singular and dual perspective forms (the nonvisual and the inferred do not). Singular perspective implies that the information was visually accessible to the speaker only, while in the case of dual perspective it is available to both the speaker and the addressee. Attested examples are in third person only. Since the language is severely endangered, it is not impossible that the system had undergone reduction due to language obsolescence (Eberhard 2018: 344–5, Telles and Wetzels 2006).

In South Conchucos Quechua, 'individual' and 'mutual' access to knowledge is distinguished for all evidential terms except the reported evidential (see Hintz and Hintz 2017, Hintz 2007: 71; Hintz 2014: 486). In contrast, Southern Nambikwara distinguishes individual and shared information source for the reported evidential, while Mamaindê makes the distinction just for the secondhand reported, but not for the thirdhand one. The forms in South Conchucos Quechua are shown in Table 6.

TABLE 6   'Individual' versus 'mutual' knowledge in
           South Conchucos Quechua evidentials

individual knowledge	direct evidential -*mi*
mutual knowledge	direct evidential -*cha:*
individual knowledge	conjecture -*chi*
mutual knowledge	conjecture -*cher*
reported information	-*shi*

In (109), -*mi* marks individual knowledge acquired through direct observation (Hintz and Hintz 2017), consistent with the semantics of -*mi*, a direct or firsthand evidential, attested across Quechuan languages: see Adelaar 2017):

(109)   Tsay-pa-*mi*   qati-ya-ra-n   *South Conchucos Quechua*
        that-GEN-DIR.INDIV   follow-PL-PAST-3
        mama-yki-kuna
        mother-2-PL
        'By that route your ancestors pastured animals' – individual knowledge

In (110), using -*cha:* implies that the speaker states her knowledge shared with a community of face-to-face interactants, that is, speech act participants.

(110)   Tsay-pa-*cha:*   qati-ya-ra-n   *South Conchucos Quechua*
        that-GEN-DIR.MUTUAL   follow-PL-PAST3
        mama-yki-kuna
        mother-2-PL
        'By that route your ancestors pastured animals' (as we all know) – shared knowledge

Sihuas Quechua, spoken in an area northwest of South Conchucos, also differentiates individual and mutual knowledge for direct and conjectural evidentials (Hintz and Hintz 2017; see also Sun 2018: 61). The forms are -*mi* 'individual direct information source', -*ma* 'collective direct information source', -*chri* 'individual inferential information source', and -*chra* 'collective inferential information source'. There is an additional distinction between two reported evidentials, -*shi* 'reported information' and -*sha* 'generalised knowledge from reported information'.

In some Quechua languages, information source and access to information are expressed separately. The markers can co-occur within one word. This is what we see in (111), from Ayacucho Quechua, where an evidential can occur with the suffix *-iki* (glossed as 'interactive'). This suffix indicates that the addressee is believed to have access to the same sources of information as the speaker themself (Soto Ruiz 1979: 199–201; Adelaar 2017: 673).

(111) yanapa-saq-m-iki,   pay   *Ayacucho Quechua*
      help-1S.FUT-ASSERT-INTERACTIVE he
      sapa   wata   yanapa-wa-n
      every year   help-10-3S
      'As you can understand, I will help him. He helps me out every year'

Knowledge sharing expressed through special evidentials appears to always involve speech act participants – speaker and addressee. So far we have no examples of special forms marking knowledge available to third person only, or to speaker and third person, but not to addressee. At this point in time, examples are too few to warrant any further generalizations.

There appear to be more examples of information sharing marked by special terms within complex evidential systems. A number of languages from Papua New Guinea appear to have special evidentials which distinguish information available just to the speaker, or to both speaker and addressee. Ekari, of the Wissel Lakes family has a form used to relate events unknown to the addressee is also used 'to report hearsay' (Doble 1987: 90, 93; Sarvasy 2018: 635). Nembi, from the Angal subgroup group of Engan, has a set of forms which distinguish the information source of speaker, addressee, or both (Tipton 1982: 78–79). Wola (Angal Heneng), from the same subgroup, appears to distinguish forms for 'both speaker and hearer witness', 'either speaker or hearer witnesses', 'hearer did not witness but heard of previously', 'speaker did not witness', and, in only the third person, 'neither speaker nor hearer witnesses (sic)' (Sillitoe 2010: 17–19; see Sarvasy 2018: 644–5 on this and other languages from this subgroup). Foe, a Kutubuan language, distinguishes the following evidential categories: 'fact known to speaker, but unseen by person spoken to'; 'seen by both speaker and addressee'; 'determined on grounds of present evidence'; 'determined on grounds of previous evidence'; and 'detected by senses' (Rule 1977: 97; Sarvasy 2018; 647). Fasu, from the same family, also appears to have suffixes which relate to the speaker and addressee's access to knowledge embedded within the system of evidentials (Loeweke and May 1980: 54–56; Sarvasy 2018: 652). For each of these, little more can be said until more comprehensive studies become available.

Sharing knowledge, shared information source, and common ground can figure among additional meanings of an evidential. This is what we turn to now.

4.3 Shared Knowledge and Shared Information Source: What Everyone Knows

Shared information, as one of the overtones of an evidential, can be based either (4.3.1) on shared information source, or (4.3.2) on the commonality of generally available knowledge.

4.3.1 Shared Information Source as Part of the Meaning of an Evidential

In many languages with evidentiality, the visual, or the direct, term is used to refer to generally known observable facts (see examples from Tariana, Quechua, and Shipibo-Konibo in Aikhenvald 2004: 167–73; see also Adelaar 2017: 673). A Tariana will use the present visual evidential for such events, such as seasonal weather phenomena (Aikhenvald 2003a: 295). An example is in (112).

(112) diha-pikeri-nuku   hĩ   kuphe paitsi   *Tariana*
       it-CL:MONTH-TOP.NON.A/S DEM.ANIM fish   frog
       na-sa-*naka*
       3pl-sing-PRES.VIS
       diha-nuku   nawiki   nhepa   na-hña-*naka*
       it-TOP.NON.A/S   people   3pl+get   3pl-eat-PRES.VIS
       'This month fish (and) frogs make noise, people get (them) and eat (them)'

The direct evidential in Quechua is used when talking about generally known facts; (113) is something every Peruvian knows (Faller 2002: 20).

(113) Yunka-pi-*n*   k'usillu-kuna-qa   ka-n   *Cuzco Quechua*
       rainforest-LOC-DIR.EV   monkey-PL-TOP   be-3p
       'In the rainforest, there are monkeys'

An evidential may express a general fact, known not to be observable by the human eye. The actions of evil spirits and supernatural activities of shamans and sorcerers are cast in nonvisual or non-witnessed evidentials (see Aikhenvald 2018a: 28–29, for a summary). (114) is a statement, in Tariana, of what an evil spirit does: as its actions cannot be seen, the general knowledge is expressed through nonvisual evidential – the commonly available information source for this kind of experience.

(114) nawiki-nuku   di-hña-*mha*   diha   *Tariana*
       people-TOP.NON.A/S 3sgnf-eat-PRES.NONVIS ART
       ñamu
       evil.spirit
       'Evil spirit eats people'

In talking about typical actions and the practices of shamans and healers, nonvisual evidential is also the preferred choice. In (115), Leonardo Brito describes what a shaman does (more examples are in Aikhenvald 2019). Shamanic dreams which lead to the diagnosis of an illness are also described with nonvisual evidential. The present nonvisual evidential is used throughout the narrative.

(115) (a) Diha-*mha*   maliẽri   tsome   maliẽri   *Tariana*
           he-PRES.NONVIS   shaman   a.lot   shaman
           alite   hiku-wani-naku
           be+CL:ANIM   appear-CL:ABSTR-TOP.NON.A/S
           nha   na-matsi-keta-mi-naku
           they   3pl-bad-THEM+CAUS-NOMIN-TOP.NON.A/S
           di-ka-*mha*   tapuli-se
           3sgnf-see-PRES.NONVIS   dream-LOC
           'The shaman sees in the dream the apparent damage made by a lot of shamans'

      (b) wheru di-eme-hyume   di-ka-*mha*
           snuff 3sgnf-sniff-SEQ:SS   3sgnf-see-PRES.NONVIS
           ne-naku.   Di-weni   nha
           then-TOP.NON.A/S   3sgnf-vengeance   they
           na-kamia-naku   di-yeneta-*mha*
           3pl-fall.ill-TOP.NON.A/S   3sgnf-pass+CAUS-PRES.NONVIS
           ne-misini-naku
           then-also-TOP.NON.A/S
           'Having snuffed snuff, he sees (it) then. Those who fall ill because of vengeance, he also makes (the illness) pass'.

The way in which an indicated person acquires shamanic powers by sniffing powerful snuff was described by the late Cândido Brito as follows:

(116) Kui   iri   hinina-mikiri-*mha*   *Tariana*
      Kui   son   penis-NOM.PAST.NF-PRES.NONVIS
      diha-naku   nha maliẽ   ne:me-*mha*   maliẽ
      he-TOP.NON.A/S   they shaman.PL 3pl+sniff-PRES.NONVIS shaman.PL
      na:-kasu   ha-ehkwapi-naku   na-yeka-kasu
      3pl+go-INT   DEM.INAN-CL:WORLD-TOP.NON.A/S 3pl-know-INT
      'The shamans sniff the type of snuff referred to as 'the cut-off penis of the son of Kui (legendary hero)', to become shamans, to know the world'

Each of these uses is associated with commonly available information sources, including what is seen or believed to be seen, and what is not.

4.3.2   Generally Available Communal Knowledge

Knowledge sharing may be expressed through an evidential whose main meaning can be described as assumption based on logical inference from general facts – something 'everyone knows'. An example comes from Tariana, a language with five-term system of evidentials. Their main function is to express information source. If the audience doubts the speaker's information source, the speaker can add justification as 'evidence' for what they are saying – for instance, adding a lexical explanation 'I saw it' to the visual evidential or 'I heard it' to the nonvisual one.

The full system of Tariana evidentials in declarative clauses was illustrated in examples (6)–(10) in section 1. All evidential markers distinguish three tenses. Just the inferred and the assumed evidential do not have present tense (we return to this section 6.1). All the evidential markers are floating clitics, and can attach to the verb or to any topical constituent within the clause (see, for instance, (120)). The forms of evidentials in three tenses in declarative clauses are listed in Table 7.

TABLE 7   Evidentials and tense in declarative clauses in Tariana

Evidentials/tenses	Present	Recent past	Remote past
Visual	-naka	-ka	-na
Nonvisual	-mha	-mahka	-mhana
Inferred	–	-nihka	-nhina
Assumed	–	-sika	-sina
Reported	-pida	-pidaka	-pidana

Evidential forms contains segmentable tense markers: the recent past marker *-ka* and the remote past marker *-na* (present forms can be considered zero-marked). There is phonological fusion on the respective boundaries (in agreement with principles described in Aikhenvald 2003a: 46–53). The visual evidential is less formally marked than others (see a comprehensive discussion of the structure of the Tariana evidentials in Aikhenvald 2003a: 289–305, and the issues of formal and functional markedness in evidential systems in Aikhenvald 2004: 70–77).

Tariana evidentials show semantic complexity, including correlations with access to knowledge. We saw in (114)–(116) that talking about supranatural phenomena requires using a nonvisual evidential. The inferred evidential is the preferred choice if the speaker had access to visual traces of an event or a state and the addressee did not, that is if information source is not shared by speech act participant. For instance, if the addressee is inside the house, and the speaker goes out and sees the rain, they will say (117) to the addressee on returning to the house. The evidential contains reference to the time of the acquisition of information, in agreement with the general meaning of tense in Tariana evidentials (see (75)–(77) in section 3.3).

(117) iya   di-hwa-*nihka*   *Tariana*
       rain   3sgnf-fall-RECENT.PAST.INFERRED
       'Rain has fallen' (inferred based on visual traces)

A brief explanation for this, in Portuguese, was 'falando para outro, ele não viu' (talking to someone else, he hasn't seen it) (see Ramirez 1997: 140, for a similar usage of inferred evidentials in Tucano).

The assumed evidential is used to express a logical assumption and common reasoning – what everyone knows based on general experience. Diká, one of the oldest speakers of the language, told an autobiographical story about how he had run into a snake while collecting rubber in the jungle. It got dark, and he could no longer see the snake, so he said (118) to himself. The nonvisual evidential reflects internal speech, or thought: Diká was alone, and not talking out loud. The story was cast in remote past, hence the remote past nonvisual.

(118) Di-a-*sika*-khani   *Tariana*
       3sgnf-go-RECENT.PAST.ASSUMED-AWAY
       nu-a-*mhana*
       1sg-say-REMOTE.PAST.NONVISUAL
       'He went away (logically assuming), I said (internally)'

The assumed evidential reflects the logical conclusion that the snake had gone away (which is what a snake was expected to do). In actual fact, the speaker turned out to be mistaken: the snake was sitting waiting for him, and he had to run up a tree to escape it. This shows that an assumption, no matter how logical, is not infallible. A brief explanation for such use in Portuguese was *só pode ser* ('can only be this').

The remote past assumed evidential is often explained, in Portuguese, as *tudo mundo sabe* ('everyone knows') – this underscores the component of shared common knowledge and tradition, by speaker, addressee, and everyone else. The basis for assumption is common sense underscored by common knowledge and shared expertise and experience.

The remote past form of the assumed evidential is the preferred choice for traditional stories relating Tariana lore – including the origin myths and accounts of the travels of the ancestors. This is similar to the way the 'general knowledge' evidential is used in Mamaindê and Southern Nambikwara (see (99) and section 4.1). A typical example is (119), from a story about the origin of potent snuff which had been given a name by Thunder (the mythical ancestor of the Tariana people).

(119) hiku-*sina*   di-keña   Tariana
       appear-ASSUMED.REMOTE.PAST   3sgnf-start
       walikasu-pu-nuku
       beginning-AUG-TOP.NON.A/S
       walikasu-pu-nuku   diha
       beginning-AUG-TOP.NON.A/S   he/it
       alia-*sina*   e:nu
       EXIST-REMOTE.PAST.ASSUMED   thunder
       kepitana-*sina*   di-na   e:nu
       REL+name-REMOTE.PAST.ASSUMED   3sgnf-OBJ   thunder
       '(It) started appearing at the very beginning (of time), it, thunder, existed at the very beginning, thunder; thunder named it'

The antiquity of the shared knowledge is reflected in the remote past component of the form. The recent past assumed evidential is never used this way.

The visual evidential – as a marker of information available through observation – and the assumed evidential – as a marker of shared communal cultural knowledge – can occur within the same story. Parts of the story about the traditional Tariana seasons are cast in visual evidential; these are the phenomena one typically observes – as shown in (112). The description of traditional naming practices and activities by the ancestors is cast in the assumed evidential: this is not something that can be observed, and belongs to the domain of shared knowledge and lore. An example is in (120): that the ancestors (the 'old people') named the Pleiades (also known as The Seven Sisters) is part of shared lore.

(120) di-pumi-se   di-yana-ka   diha   walipere   *Tariana*
      3sgnf-after-LOC   3sgnf-pass-SEQ   it   Pleiades
      diha-*sina*   pedalia-pe   nepitaneta
      it-ASSUMED.REMOTE.PAST   old-PL   3pl+name+CAUS
      'After it (previous month) passes, Pleiades, old people named them'

The assumed evidential is used by representatives of all generations of speakers to talk about what they had read (all of the extant speakers, except for two elders, are functionally literate), and in translations. A popular Brazilian song 'Dois patinhos na lagoa começaram à nadar' (Two ducklings in a lake started swimming) was translated by Rafael Brito, one of the youngest speakers, using the assumed evidential. The first line of the song goes like this (121):

(121) ñhamepa   kumada-tupe   kalisana-dawa-se
      two+CL:HUMAN   duck-PL.DIM   lake-CL:HOLE-LOC
      na-yha   na-keña-*sina*
      3pl-swim   3pl-start-REM.P.ASSUM
      'Two ducklings in a lake started swimming'

Example (122) comes from a translation of a Catholic prayer (called 'Oração da família cristã', prayer for a Christian family).

(122) Kurusatai-se   Yapirikuri   di-sata-*sina*   *Tariana*
      cross-LOC   Jesus   3sgnf-ask-REM.P.ASSUM
      diha   hado-nuku   wa-na   duhua   wha   hado
      he   mother-TOP.NON.A/S   1pl-OBJ she   we   mother
      kayu   du-kakwani-karu   du-enipe-nuku
      like   3sgf-look.after-PURP   3sgf-children-TOP.NON.A/S
      'On the cross Jesus asked his mother to look after us in the same way as a mother looks after her children'[14]

---

14   The original is *Na cruz Jesús pediu a sua mãe de cuidar de nós como uma mãe cuida dos seus filhos.*

Only those elders who consider themselves well-versed in the centuries-old knowledge and lore (and are considered so by others) venture to tell traditional stories cast in assumed evidentials. There is thus a correlation between the status of a person within the community, their knowledgeability (acknowledged by them and by others) and the use of the assumed evidential referring to 'shared knowledge'.

The correlation between evidential conventions and type of stories is shared with a few East Tukanoan languages of the area, with which Tariana is in constant contact. In Desano, 'the assumed evidential with past tense is most often used for legends' (Miller 1999: 67). Along similar lines, speakers of Wanano/Kotiria use the assumed evidential for traditional stories 'in which they take on the role of a narrator', 'being the conduit for shared, collective knowledge' (Stenzel and Gomez-Imbert 2018: 383). The Wanano/Kotiria are traditional marriage partners of the Tariana. There is no traditional intermarriage between the Desano and the Tariana, as they are believed to be classificatory siblings (see Aikhenvald 2003a for further details).

In contrast, tales and stories which do not have any particular significance or import are told using the remote past reported (or hearsay) evidential, in all these languages, including Tariana. In Miller's (1999: 67) words, 'the hearsay evidential is [...] used, especially by the younger generation hearing the stories from other people'.

The usage of the assumed evidential in traditional stories is reminiscent of the general knowledge evidential in Nambikwara languages (as we can recall from section 4.1, based on Eberhard 2018: 353). The assumed evidential reflects the lore and the heritage accessible to every member of the Tariana community.

The assumed evidential in Tariana and in neighbouring languages is semantically complex: it refers to

(a) assumptions based on logical reasoning (available to anyone who can reason);
(b) the information available to everyone (including reading and translations); and
(c) traditional stories, as part of shared cultural heritage.

As the Tariana language and the people's traditional lore become obsolescent, the balance of the assumed evidential in its various usages undergoes change. The assumed evidential is used by representatives of all generations of speakers to talk about what they had read (all of the extant speakers are functionally literate), and in translations. But those elders who would be knowledgeable enough to tell traditional stories cast in assumed evidential are getting to be fewer and fewer. Younger and less knowledgeable speakers retell such stories using the reported evidential (explaining, if asked, that this is what they had heard from their elders). The use of the remote past assumed evidential for shared knowledge and important lore is on the wane.

General knowledge may be part of the meaning of other forms, evidentials among them. Tundra Nenets, a Samoyedic language, has a special 'prospective' evidential, which marks future prediction based on general knowledge (Skribnik and Kehayov 2018: 549–550). In Darma, a West Himalayish language (Willis 2007, 2019), 'general knowledge' is part of the meaning of the indirect evidential (other terms in the system are direct/visual, inferred and reported; see also Hyslop 2018b: 602).[15] In all such instances, just one evidential term extends into the semantic domain of egophoricity.

5 Unequal Relations between Evidentiality and Epistemic Modality

Evidentiality and epistemic modality interact. Evidentials can have epistemic overtones – this is what we saw under B in sections 2.2 and 2.7, and examples (21)–(23). Epistemic modalities may develop overtones of non-firsthand information, covering inference and hearsay, as we saw in G, and example (29), and thus constitute evidentiality strategies. Further instances of epistemic extensions of evidentials and evidential extensions of epistemic modalities are discussed by Wiemer (2018: 91–95). We can recall, from Table 3, that epistemic modality and evidentiality share two features – variable scope (section 3.1) and also the possibility of double marking (section 3.2). None of these are shared with egophoricity and mirativity.

Grammaticalization paths point towards an asymmetrical relationship between epistemic modality and evidentiality. Historical development of evidentials follows two general paths (see also Aikhenvald 2021a, Friedman 2018, Mélac 2014, 2019).[16] Firstly, markers of evidentiality may develop out of grammaticalizing a lexical item: a verb, or, less frequently, a noun becomes a grammatical marker of information source within a closed system of choices. Secondly, an evidential may evolve out of an evidentiality strategy via reinterpretation, acquiring the status of a marker of information source par

---

15   See also Gipper (2014), on how the addressee's knowledge is relevant for the use of reported and inferential evidentials in Yurakaré, an isolate from Bolivia. An evidentially unmarked form within a small system may express general or common knowledge (see Wojtylak 2018: 395, 401 on Murui and Bora).
16   In Kurtöp, a Tibeto-Burman language, miratives stem from reinterpretation of clause-chaining constructions and of clausal nominalizations (see Hyslop 2020). Not enough information is available on patterns of grammaticalization of mirativity or egophoricity across the world, to offer any generalizations.

excellence. Such evidentiality strategies often include epistemic modalities. In numerous instances across the world, an epistemic modality may acquire overtones of uncertain and non-firsthand information, and then develop into a non-firsthand evidential – see section 6.2, for some examples from Abkhaz and Circassian, two Northwest Caucasian languages, Akha, and Hill Patwin. In Cree/Montagnais/Naskapi, an Algonquian language from Canada, conjunct dubitative forms have developed non-firsthand evidential meanings (see James, Clarke and MacKenzie 2001: 230; 254–7, Junker et al. 2018). The hearsay evidential in Wintu appears to have originated in a morpheme meaning 'maybe, potentially' (Schlichter 1986). And in Tariana, the assumed evidential originated in a marker of dubitative modality (Aikhenvald 2021a).

The development and grammaticalization of epistemic modalities takes a different direction. Just like any other category, markers of epistemic modalities may originate from independent lexical items. The lexeme meaning 'get, receive, obtain' may give rise to markers of possibility (see Kuteva et al. 2019: 191). Markers of epistemic modality are known to evolve as a result of reinterpretation of other modal categories. Examples include the development of future to probability (Kuteva et al. 2019: 185), and of markers of ability to those of probability (Kuteva et al. 2019: 346; see also Ziegeler 2011).

In the course of the history of healthy languages, exponents of epistemic modality never come from reinterpretation of evidentials. Developments in this direction are only known to occur in the situation of language obsolescence.

Wintu is a case in point. The system of evidentials in the traditional language recorded by Dorothy D. Lee in the 1930s consisted of five terms: visual, nonvisual sensory, inferential ('information inferred from logic applied to circumstantial sensory evidence': Pitkin 1984: 133–4), experiential ('information deduced from experience' which 'involves the exercise of judgement': Pitkin 1984: 134), and reported (Pitkin 1984: 147 and Lee 1938, 1944). A reduced system with just two choices – visual sensory and reported – had survived by the time Pitkin did his fieldwork on the Wintu language in the 1950s. The visual evidential replaced the nonvisual in a few contexts, including descriptions of one's feelings. Talking about a headache in 1930 would have involved the nonvisual sensory -nt^{h}ere, while a quarter of a century later the same statement involved a visual evidential (Pitkin 1984: 150).

The two remaining evidentials have strong epistemic overtones, of certainty versus doubt (see Pitkin 1984: 152). The shift may have occurred under pressure from English. This goes together with the fact that an endangered language tends to restructure their grammatical systems to 'match' those of the dominant majority language which is gradually replacing it.

The other scenario whereby the use of modals stems from the use of evidentials comes from attempts at rendering them into another language. Exponents of evidentiality are hard to translate into languages which lack the category. In many familiar Indo-European languages, including English, meanings related to 'information source' can be expressed through lexical means – including verbs of perception or cognition – and a closed class of modal verbs, such as *may, might* or *must*. Can – but don't have to. Translation from languages with evidentials into English, Portuguese, Spanish and many others often involves epistemic modals, for want of other means. This has led some scholars to the conclusion that evidentials are 'epistemic modals' because this is how they are translated into English (as has been recently claimed by Matthewson et al. 2007, Peterson 2018, and earlier by Palmer 1986, to name just a few of those who prefer 'analysing' translational short-cuts to undertaking an in-depth analysis of each linguistic system).

Speakers of Tariana, Tucano and other languages within the Vaupés River Basin linguistic area in Brazil have their own ethnolect of Portuguese. One of their features is the use of lexical equivalents for evidentiality markers (obligatory in their original languages, as we saw above, for Tariana). These lexical ways of marking information source allow speakers to conform to social conventions of being precise in stating the source of knowledge, so as to avoid accusations of incompetence, or sorcery.

Tariana has five evidentials – visual, nonvisual, inferred, assumed and reported. When the Tariana speak Portuguese, statements referring to information obtained visually is usually accompanied by a phrase *eu vi* 'I saw', or (if contrasted to something else) *eu tenho prova* 'I have proof'; or, more rarely, *eu tenho experiência* 'I have experience' (see also section 3.6).

Both expressions 'I have proof' and 'I have experience' are also used to translate the inferred evidential. Information obtained by hearing or by other sensory experience can be accompanied by *eu escutei* 'I heard' or *eu senti* 'I felt', matching the nonvisual evidential. The formula *diz que* 'it is said that' is a conventional way of marking reported information. The assumed evidential is translated with a modal verb, *parece* 'it appears, it seems' (Aikhenvald 2004: 298, 2018b: 164–8). This verb is used in oral translations into Portuguese, including the rendering of what one has just read. An announcement about an upcoming football match in the community was rephrased, in the Vaupés Portuguese, as 'there is a football match at 5 o'clock on Monday, *parece* (it appears)'.

Such uses provoke adverse reaction among non-Indian Brazilians – as if Indians were incredulous or did not use the language properly.[17] A modal verb is used as a resource to translate an evidential – whose real meaning

---

17   Along the lines of linguistic misunderstandings between the Valle Verde Yavapai and Anglos in the USA based on the use of evidentials, described by Bunte and Kendall (1981).

of assumed, inferred, and shared information source is well and truly lost in translation.

Along similar lines. Elsa Gomez-Imbert's main consultant of Tatuyo, an East Tukanoan language spoken on the Colombian side of the same Vaupés River Basin Linguistic area as Tariana, 'also tried to compensate for the lack of evidentials in Spanish with lexical expressions, and was happy to learn of the existence of a reportative expression *dizque*, which she incorporated into her elementary Spanish' (Stenzel and Gomez-Imbert 2018: 382).

The relationship between evidentiality and epistemic modality is unequal. An exponent of epistemic modality may give rise to an evidential term within a system (but never all the terms in a multiterm system). Examples the other way around – from an evidential to an epistemic modal – are restricted to specific situations of language obsolescence and of translation into a language without grammatical evidentials.

6 Dependencies between Evidentiality and Other Grammatical Categories

Choices made within an evidentiality system may depend on grammatical categories of other kinds, in terms of the meanings expressed. The principles of regular dependencies between grammatical categories, or grammatical systems, have been developed in Aikhenvald and Dixon (2011). There, we considered relationships between polarity, reference classification (covering gender and classifiers of various kinds), tense, aspect, person, number, case, with a number of tentative dependencies involving evidentiality. Dependencies form a hierarchy, with polarity occupying the top position (Aikhenvald and Dixon 2011: 196). This implies that the choice made in any grammatical category will depend on whether the clause or a sentence is negative or not. In agreement with this principle, one finds fewer distinctions in evidentiality, tense, aspect, and other categories made in negative than in positive clauses. The ways in which evidentiality interrelates with other categories were further discussed in Aikhenvald (2015a). This was based on a larger selection of languages and new systems described, and how evidentials interrelate with other categories, both clausal and nominal. Our discussion here offers a logical progression of this investigation, based on further data.

Links between evidentiality and other categories can be of SYNCHRONIC or of DIACHRONIC nature. Synchronically, the expression of evidentiality can be fused with another category. We can recall, from section 2, that in Jarawara evidentiality is fused with tense and with gender. Exponents of evidentiality may have special meanings in the context of other categories. We will see in section 6.1 that a reported or a speculative evidential may acquire an overtone of politeness in the context of a command. Our focus here is on correlations between the choice of an evidential within the context of other categories. In other words, we focus on how the choice of evidentiality values may depend on choices made within another category. For instance, fewer evidentiality values are usually expressed in non-declarative sentences. Diachronic links between categories and their documented developments in language history may provide a partial explanation for their synchronic dependencies.

A further formal, kind of interaction between evidentials and other clausal (or verbal) categories can be reflected in the slot which evidentials occupy in the verbal word, and their paradigmatic relations with other categories. In many languages (e.g. Yukaghir (isolate), Archi and a few other Nakh-Daghestanian languages, Samoyedic (Uralic), and Wakashan) evidentials occupy the same slot in the verbal word as do exponents of mood and are mutually exclusive with these (more examples and references are in Aikhenvald 2004: 241–2, 2015a: 243). There are thus no evidentiality distinctions in non-declarative moods. A typological investigation of the position of evidential markers within a verbal word goes beyond the scope of this study.

In section 6.1, we turn to the dependencies attested so far between evidentiality and clausal or sentential categories. Diachronic links between evidentiality and other categories which partly provide motivation for the attested dependencies are the topic of section 6.2. In section 6.3 we address the expression of non-propositional evidentiality – that is, grammaticalised information source encoded within a noun phrase in its scope – and some categories it may relate to. Brief conclusions are in section 6.4.

6.1 Dependencies between Evidentiality, and Clausal and Sentential Categories

The choices available in the evidentiality system may correlate with, and depend on, choices made in (6.1.1) the tense system, (6.1.2) the aspect system, (6.1.5) mood, or sentence type, (6.1.6) polarity, (6.1.4) types of clauses, (6.1.3) modality and (6.1.7) person and number.

6.1.1 Evidentiality Depends on Tense: Tense > Evidentiality[18]

In numerous languages of the world, the maximum number of evidential specifications is found in past tenses. In Hinuq, Tatar, Jarawara and Matses

---

18 This notation follows Aikhenvald and Dixon (2011) which discusses dependencies mentioned here under (6.1.1) and (6.1.7). Other dependencies involving evidentials are not addressed in Aikhenvald and Dixon (2011). The sign > indicates the direction of dependency.

evidentiality is distinguished exclusively in past tenses (see also the general discussion of Nakh-Daghestanian languages by Forker 2018, and studies of individual languages, including Agul, by Maisak and Merdanova 2002, and Lezgi by Greed 2017[19]). The choices made in the tense system thus determine the choices made in the system of evidentials.

There may be fewer evidential distinctions in non-past tenses than in past tenses. Tuyuca, an East Tukanoan language (Barnes 1984), has five evidentiality choices – visual; nonvisual; apparent; secondhand or reported; and assumed – in past tense. There are just four choices in present tense: this has 'no secondhand evidential'. No evidentiality specification can be made in future tense. Tucano (Ramirez 1997: 120) distinguishes four evidentials – visual, nonvisual, inferred and reported – in the recent past and in the remote past tenses. Only visual and nonvisual distinctions are made in the present tense, and none in the future. This pattern is similar to other East Tukanoan languages (Stenzel and Gomez-Imbert 2018): there is typically no present tense specification for reported, inferred, or assumed evidential.

In Tariana five evidentiality distinctions (visual, nonvisual, inferred, assumed and reported) are made in the two past tenses (recent past and remote past). Only three distinctions – visual, nonvisual and reported – are made in the present tense – see Table 7, and also examples (6)–(10). The present reported evidential -*pida* is used similarly to a quotative marker, to report something that has just been said. Examples of the recent past and the remote past reported forms are in (75)–(76). In (124), -*pida* is used as a quotative marker: a younger speaker repeats what an older speaker has just said, about a placename in (123).

(123)   Inari-na-*naka*   *Tariana: an older speaker*
        mucura.rat-CL.VERT-PRES.VIS
        'It is The hill of mucura rat (visual)'

(124)   Inari-na-*pida*   *Tariana: a younger speaker repeating*
        mucura.rat-CL.VERT-PRES.REP
        'It is The hill of mucura rat (present reported)'

---

19   Greed's (2017) paper is based on firsthand fieldwork with speakers of Lezgi, a member of the Lezgic branch of Nakh-Daghestanian languages. It contains a comprehensive analysis of the expression of direct and indirect (or non-firsthand) evidential distinctions through various means in the language, most of which were overlooked by Haspelmath's (1993) grammar of the language based on published materials and only limited access to the speaker community.

The present reported evidential can also be used to report something one has just heard. In (125), Jovino is reporting the information conveyed to him by phone a few minutes before.

(125) Kuite   nu-dakiri   Eberti-nuku   *Tariana*
      what's.name+CL.ANIM 1sg-grandson Evert-TOP.NON.A/S
      ma-pisa-de-*pida*
      NEG-cut-NEG-PRES.REP
      'They didn't operate on, what's (his) name, my grandson Ebert' (I was told a few minutes ago)

In its quotative usage, the Tariana form -*pida* is similar to its cognate in Baniwa of Içana (example (2)), which combines a reported and a quotative meaning. The difference is that Baniwa of Içana has only one, reported, evidential form, with no tense distinctions, and Tariana has five evidential terms with different sets of tenses. The development of a multi-term evidential system and of tense distinctions in Tariana evidentials is the result of areal diffusion from East Tukanoan languages (mechanisms and sources were described in Aikhenvald 2004: 285–7).

Further dependencies of evidentiality on tense have been found in multi-term systems in Nambikwara languages. Present, recent past, intermediate past, and distant past in Mamaindê are distinguished in visual, nonvisual, inferred and the secondhand reported evidentiality. No tense distinctions are made in thirdhand reported and general knowledge evidentials (see Table 4). Southern Nambikwara offers a somewhat more complex dependency. Present, recent past and past are distinguished in visual and inferred evidentials. Recent past, past and remote past are distinguished in the reported evidential. No tenses are distinguished in the general knowledge evidential (see Table 5).

This direction of dependency is intuitively plausible. An information source reflects something already perceived and taken in by the speaker. This is especially so if we have to deal with non-firsthand information, inference, assumption, and also verbal report. The lack of tense in general evidentials in the two Nambikwara languages correlates with timeless character of general knowledge available to everyone.

Southern Nambikwara offers an additional dependency between evidentiality, tense, and individual or dual information sharing. Within the reported specification, three tenses – recent past, past, and remote past – are distinguished for individual perspective (reflecting the knowledge of one person). Just two – recent past and past – are distinguished for 'dual' perspective, that is, information shared between speaker and addressee. Individual versus dual perspective are not expressed within the general knowledge evidential: this is what is shown in Table 5 (see Eberhard 2018, for additional points on the correlations of access to information, tense and evidentials in Lakondê, a highly endangered Nambikwara language for which only partial data are available). These dependencies reflect the semantic features of information sharing and access to information built into evidential systems, and will be well worth a separate study once more information on the interrelations between access to information and other categories become available.

Future, in many languages including those mentioned in this section, has strong epistemic meanings, of uncertainty and is not compatible with information source (see also 6.1.3 below, and Fleck 2007 on Matses).

A number of languages where evidentiality is expressed in future show a dependency of evidentiality on tense. Foe, an East Kutubuan language from Papua New Guinea (Sarvasy 2018: 646–50), has future forms just for a visual evidential, an inferred evidential based on previously visible results, and an inferred evidential based on currently visible results. In Sabanê, a Nambikwara language, inferred evidential lacks a future and a present form, while a sensory evidential has three tense forms (past, present, and future). No tense is expressed in the reported evidential (Eberhard 2018: 347–8). In Kalmyk (Skribnik and Seesing 2014: 153), only the inferred and reported evidentials are distinguished within future forms, while assumed evidential distinguishes present and past. Direct and indirect terms have only past reference. Additional difficulties with investigating future distinctions within evidential systems have to do with a problematic status of future as a modality or a tense. A combination of future with an evidential may result in creating combinations with epistemic meanings. For instance, a combination of future and inferred evidential in Ersu marks probability, rather than information source (Zhang 2016: 589).

6.1.2(a)   Evidentiality Depends on Aspect: Aspect > Evidentiality

The choice of evidentials may depend on the choice made in the aspect system. Evidential distinctions made in perfective aspect in Kurtöp, a Tibeto-Burman language from Bhutan, cover personal knowledge versus lack thereof, and shared versus non-shared knowledge (Hyslop 2014a, b). Only expectation of knowledge is distinguished within the imperfective aspect. Evidentiality is expressed only within perfective aspect in Lhasa Tibetan (Tibeto-Burman: DeLancey 1986: 210–11, 2003: 278),[20] and Georgian (South-Caucasian: Comrie

---

20   Other studies in tense-aspect systems of Tibetan varieties, including Zeisler (2011) and Tournadre (2004, 2011), do not clearly focus on interrelationships between evidentiality and perfective and imperfective values.

1976: 110). In Barasano and Tatuyo, two East Tukanoan languages spoken in Colombia, nonvisual perception is marked only within imperfective aspect (perfective aspect offers fewer choices in evidentials) (Gomez-Imbert 2014).

6.1.2(b)   Aspect Depends on Evidentiality: Evidentiality > Aspect
In the opposite direction, a choice made in another system may depend on the choice made in the evidentiality system. The choices available in a combined Tense/Aspect system may depend on the choice that is made in the Evidentiality system. In Kashaya (Pomoan: Oswalt 1986: 37), the aspectual distinctions (perfective versus imperfective) are not expressed in auditory and inferential evidentials. Other evidentials (visual, quotative and performative) have this distinction. Bulgarian (Slavic) has a grammatical system combining Tense, Aspect and Evidentiality; this has nine choices available in non-reported but just five in reported evidentiality; so, for instance, present and imperfect fall together, as do perfect and past perfect, and future perfect and past future perfect (based on the analysis by Scatton 1984: 319, 330–1; see also Jakobson 1971 and Friedman 1986).

6.1.3   Modality Depends on Evidentiality: Modality > Evidentiality
Various non-declarative epistemic and also deontic modalities – conditional, dubitative, obligational and so on – allow fewer evidential specifications than the indicative. This is so because in many languages – including Matses (Fleck 2007) – information source is irrelevant for statements which are epistemic in nature and for statements about the future (which may be considered on a par with modality). In Estonian the reported evidential does not occur with the conditional modality. In !Xun (König 2013) evidentials do not occur with any modality.

However, this is not a steadfast rule. In some languages, including Tarma Quechua (Adelaar 1977: 98–9), all evidentials can occur together with modality markers. The non-firsthand evidential in Abkhaz does not occur with debitive, conditional, optative or intentional because they occupy the same slot within the verb. The evidential can occur together with the potential marker, with the meaning of inference and potentiality of action (Chirikba 2003: 252–4).

6.1.4   Evidentiality Depends on Clause Types: Clause Type > Evidentiality
In many languages, evidentials are not expressed in non-main clauses (including complement clauses, relative clauses, and temporal subordinate clauses). Examples of languages in which evidentials cannot appear in dependent clauses of any sort include Matses (Panoan: Fleck 2007), Tariana (Arawak: Aikhenvald 2003a), Tucano (East Tukanoan: Ramirez 1997), Cavineña (Tacanan: Guillaume 2008), Hinuq (North-East Caucasian: Forker 2013, 2014), Tatar (Turkic:

Greed 2014) and Kalmyk (Mongolic: Skribnik and Seesing 2014). For all of these languages, it can be argued that evidentials are expressed on the sentence-level only, that is, the marking of information source has sentential scope and appears on the main clause within a complex sentence.

The examples of languages where a non-main clause can be within the scope of an evidential come exclusively from languages with small evidential systems – this is what we saw in (53), from Jarawara, (54)–(56), from Estonian, and (57), from Bulgarian (see also Aikhenvald 2004: 253–6). It appears, however, that even in these languages not all non-main clauses can have their own evidentiality specification. We can recall, from (56), that temporal and factual conditional clauses in Estonian only occasionally have their own evidentiality specification (different from that of the main clause) (Petar Kehayov, p.c.). We can recall, from section 3.1.2, that relative clauses in Jarawara are the among the few kinds of dependent clause in which evidential distinctions are consistently made (see example (53)). Instances of other dependent clauses with their own tense-evidentiality marking in Jarawara are limited to the situations when 'the main clause relates to present time (and thus has no tense-modal suffix) but the dependent clause relates to past time' (Dixon 2004: 470). The expression of evidentiality in non-main clauses is thus restricted, compared to what we find for main clauses. This confirms the direction of the dependency of evidentiality on clause type.

6.1.5 Evidentiality Depends on Sentence Type: Sentence Type > Evidentiality

Just like most other grammatical categories, evidentials interrelate with mood, or sentence type (that is, declarative, interrogative, imperative, and also exclamative). The maximum number of evidential specifications tends to be distinguished in declarative main clauses. Exclamative clauses in Tariana and Tucano contain no evidentials. In Shilluk, a Western Nilotic language with three evidentials (firsthand, inferred, and reported), only the firsthand evidential occurs in exclamations (Miller and Gilley 2007: 197).

A reduced system of evidentials is typical for commands. Cross-linguistically speaking, the most frequent evidential in commands is reported (meaning 'do what someone else told you to': see Aikhenvald 2010: 138–141; see also examples from Shipibo-Konibo, in Valenzuela 2003: 42, and Saaroa in Pan 2018: 666–7). Tariana and many neighbouring Tukanoan languages with four to five evidential terms in statements are no exception (see Aikhenvald 2008 on the expression of commands in these languages): the only evidential in imperative clauses is reported. An example of such a reported, or 'secondhand', command, from Tariana, is in (126).

(126) karaka   pi-merita-*pida*!   *Tariana*
       chicken   2sg-fry-REPORTED.IMPERATIVE
       'Fry the chicken (someone else told you to, the speaker is reporting this command)!'

The cognate form -*pida* in Baniwa of Içana (see (2)) is not used in commands in its reported meaning. It can be used to quote a command produced by someone else, as shown in (127) (author's own work). One person said *pi-pídzo* (2sg-sweep) 'you sweep'!', and the other repeated it as (127), to make sure I write this down properly, with no overtone of a command by proxy:

(127) pi-pídzo-*pida*   *Baniwa of Içana*
       2sg-sweep-REP
       'You sweep (repeating what someone else said)'

In just a few languages – including the isolates Maidu (Shipley 1964: 51) and Nivkh (Gruzdeva 2001: 70) – firsthand evidentiality is expressed in commands. In Tariana, a visual versus nonvisual distinction is made in apprehensive forms with the meaning of warning 'lest, beware of, or else' (Aikhenvald 2003a: 384). There are two apprehensive enclitics, -*da* 'visual apprehensive' and -*ñhina* 'nonvisual apprehensive'. The nonvisual apprehensive is used mostly with second person and only rarely with third person, and implies that, according to the speaker, the addressee cannot see what he or she is doing, or the speaker cannot see what the addressee is doing.

Someone who is walking in front can say (128) to a person behind them who might be not cautious enough, using the nonvisual apprehensive form.

(128) nu-pumi pi-pinita mẽda   pi-wha-ñhina   *Tariana*
       1sg-after 2sg-follow COUNTEREXP 2sg-fall-APPREH.NONVIS
       'Do follow me, or else you might fall down (you are not looking).'

The visual apprehensive will be used if the addressee is known to have visual access to what they are supposed to be warned against, as in (129).

(129) pi-ka-nha   ka-kolo-ka-whya   di-nu-ka
       2sg-see-SUGGESTION   REL-roll-THEM-CL:CANOE   3sgnf-come-SUB
       wa-na   di-pasya-da
       1pl-OBJ 3sgnf-smash-APPREH.NONVIS
       'Please look, when the car comes, lest it might squash us.'

Baraby (2017) argues that Innu, an Algonquian language, expresses indirect or non-firsthand evidentiality in commands (not just in statements). The indirect imperative 'targets a fulfilment of the order in the absence of the speaker', 'providing the context for the absence of the speaker who will not witness the action s/he ordered'. An example is in (130).

(130) 'Muk^u tshin tshiue-*me*,'   nitau,   *Innu*
       just   you   go.back-2sg.INDIRECT.IMP, I.tell.him,
       "kute   nin   nika   tanaukue"
       here   me   I.will stay
       I told him/her: 'Go back by yourself, me, I am going to stay here.'

This meaning is typical for the indirect, or non-firsthand, evidential throughout the language (Junker et al. 2018: 443).

In a number of languages, fewer evidential choices are available in interrogative clauses than in statements. In Mamaindê evidentials are restricted to declaratives only (Eberhard 2009: 471–6). In Shipibo-Konibo, a Panoan language, with four evidentials (visual, nonvisual, assumed and reported), only the assumed evidential -*mein* is used in questions of all types (Valenzuela 2003: 47–9). In (131), it occurs in a content question. After students had read a story about a man having killed forty red monkeys who had eaten up his bananas, the teacher asked the students (131).

(131) Jaweti   joshin shino-*mein*   joni-n   *Shipibo-Konibo*
       how.many   red   monkey.ABS-ASSUM   man-ERG
       rete-a   iki?
       kill-COMPLETIVE.PARTICIPLE   AUX
       'How many red monkeys did the man kill?'

In Bora (Bora-Witotoan: Thiesen and Weber 2012: 321, Wojtylak 2018: 403) only the reported evidential occurs in questions, while visual and nonvisual terms do not. In (132), the reported evidential is used to inquire about the reported information learnt from a third party, not the person who the question is addressed to.

(132) à-βà   ú́   pʰɛ̀-ɛ́-ʔì   *Bora*
       INTER-REP   2sg   go-FUT-CL
       'Is it true (as someone told me) that you will go?'

In contrast, in Eastern Pomo (Pomoan), in Tariana and in Tucano, all evidentials, except the reported, occur in questions (see McLendon 2003, Ramirez 1997: 144, Aikhenvald 2003a: 311–18).[21]

The meanings of evidentials in questions may differ from those in statements (see Aikhenvald 2018a: 20–3). An evidential may reflect the speaker's information source in questions, as in Eastern Pomo (McLendon 2003: 114–16). In (133), the question contains the nonvisual sensory evidential -(i)nk'e. The speaker heard the sneeze but does not know who it who was sneezed.

(133) kiyá=t'a   ʔeč-*ink'e*   *Eastern Pomo*
       who=INTER   sneeze-SENSORY.EVIDENTIAL
       'Who sneezed?' (speaker heard the sneeze but does not know who sneezed)

Alternatively, an evidential may reflect the information source of the addressee, as in Tariana and Tucano, and also Middle Mongolian, in Khalkha, Kalmyk and Monguor (see also Aikhenvald 2004: 245–7; Brosig and Skribnik 2018). Example (134), from Tariana, is a question by the Creator whose son was killed through negligence of a nasty relative asks the relative where the son is gone. The Creator is omniscient: he had seen what had happened to his son. The question here sounds as an accusation.

(134) nuri   kani-nihka   di-a   diha   *Tariana*
       1sg+son   where-INTER.PAST.VIS   3sgnf-go   he
       'My son, where is he gone'?' (the speaker saw the event)

In Philippine languages, a polar interrogative with a reported evidential may be used by the speaker 'seeking to know something that the addressee has learned from some source' (Daguman 2018: 684–5, for examples from Tagalog and Northern Kankanay). Or an evidential in questions may also reflect the information source of a third party – someone other than Speech Act Participants (see Aikhenvald 2004: 248). This is a feature of Murui, a Witotoan language (Wojtylak 2018: 394–400), a few Turkic languages (Johanson 2018: 521), and Tsou (Pan 2018: 672). Content and polar questions may differ as to whose information source they reflect. In Mari, a Finno-Ugric language, evidentials in content questions reflect the information source of the addressee, and those in

---

21 Evidentials available in statements and questions in Barasano, Tatuyo, and Wanano appear to reflect different sets of reality status and aspect combinations (Stenzel and Gomez-Imbert 2018: 379–80).

a polar question reflect the information source of the speaker (Skribnik and Kehayov 2018: 536, 538). In (135), from a description of the traditional eating habits of the Mari people, the questioner expects non-firsthand knowledge of the answerer.

(135) Marij-vlak šošəm mo-gaj šür-əm   *Mari*
      Mari-PL in_spring what-kind soup-ACC
      šolt-*en*-ât?
      cook-PAST.UNWITNESSED-3PL
      'What kind of soup did Maris cook in the spring?' (the questioner expects a non-firsthand evidential in the answer from the addressee)

In (136), the questioner has non-firsthand information that the addressee has been shooting. The choice of the evidential is determined by the information source available to the questioner, not the answerer.

(136) Təj lüjəlt-*ən*-at?   *Mari*
      you shoot-PAST.UNWITNESSED-2SG
      'Did you shoot?'

Further discussion of the information source in questions, and references, are in Aikhenvald (2018a: 20–22).

A reported evidential can occur in a question if the question is quoted by another person, or asked on behalf of someone else (much like a reported command discussed above, with an example from Tariana in (126)). This is how the reported evidential *-pida* is used in questions in Baniwa of Içana. During my stay in the village of Santa Terezinha in 2012, my adopted brother asked a shy little girl (137).

(137) kwaka pi:pitana?   *Baniwa of Içana*
      what 2sg+name
      'What's your name?'

The girl demurred. Her mother repeated the question using the reported evidential *-pida* in (138).

(138) kwaka pi:pitana-*pida*?
      what 2sg+name-REP
      'What's your name?' – reported/quotative(meaning: he asked you what your name is)

We can recall, from (2), that the evidential *-pida* in declarative clauses in Baniwa of Içana has a reportative and a quotative meaning. Both meanings occur in interrogative clauses. In contrast, commands have just the quotative meaning.

A similar instance of the reported evidential in Saaroa (Pan 2018: 666) is illustrated in (139). The speaker is talking 'on behalf of someone else to direct the question to the addressee (second person)' (see also Pan 2015: 355).

(139) um-a-usalhʉ=i=*ami*   maataata?   *Saaroa*
       AV-IRR-rain=Q=REP   tomorrow
       '(He or she wants to know) will it rain tomorrow?'

This is the only evidential which can occur in questions (the other evidential, the assumed =*'ai*, appears not to).

The reported evidential *kunu* in Ilonggo, a Philippine language, also has a quotative function in questions (Daguman 2018: 677–8). This is shown in (140).

(140) ʔanu   ʔaŋ   kinahaŋlan   niya   *kunu*?   *Ilonggo*
       what   ABS   need   3SG.GEN   REP
       'What did she say she needed?'

In (141), from Boi'nun, another Philippine language, the reported evidential can be used in a question asked on behalf of another person (Daguman 2018: 685).

(141) Taga-sari   *kono*   ʔika?   *Boi'nun*
       from-where   REP   2SG.ABS
       'Where are you from?' (Meaning: someone is asking this; I am reporting the question on their behalf)

In these examples, reported evidential in an interrogative clause has a somewhat different meaning attested in a declarative clause.

In a number of instances, a reported evidential in a non-declarative clause has an overtone of politeness, expressing a 'softer', or a 'politer' command. In Cavineña, a Tacanan language from Bolivia, the second position reportative clitic =*pa* can be used to 'soften' a command (it can also be used just to report someone else's order: Guillaume 2008: 185, 646). An example is in (142).

(142) Jeti=kwe=*pa*!   Ba-diru-kwe=*pa*!   *Cavineña*
       come-IMP.SG=REP   see-go.permissive-IMP.SG=REP
       '(Daddy) come over, he says! Go see him, he says!'

Similar overtones of the reported evidentials in commands were described for Warlpiri and Arrernte, Australian languages (Laughren 1982: 138; Wilkins 1989: 393). In (143), from Mparntwe Arrernte, the reported evidential *kwele* is used to 'soften' a command:

(143)   Arrantherre *kwele* ntert-irr-Ø-aye!   *Mparntwe Arrernte*
        2plSubject   REP   quiet-INCH-IMP-EMPH
        'You mob are supposed to be quiet (lit. Someone else has said that you mob have to shut up!)'

Along similar lines, in Brokpa, a Bodish (Tibeto-Burman) language from Bhutan, the reported evidential =*se* in imperative clauses functions as a marker of a polite command (Wangdi forthcoming: Chapter 14). The reported evidential within a question in Tsou has an overtone of politeness, as shown in (144) (Pan 2018: 672, Pan 2015: 356). This is a polite request for a permission.

(144)   te-'o   *nana* peel-a   an-a   'e   huv'o   eni?   *Tsou*
        IRR-1SG REP   able-PTV eat-PTV NOM.VIS   tangerine this
        'May I eat this tangerine?'

By using the reported evidential, a command is attributed to someone other than the speaker. This makes the command less direct and less imposing, allowing the speaker (that is, the one who is 'commanding') to be less face-threatening (in the sense of Brown and Levinson 1987) and thus sound politer and more deferential.

In Shipibo-Konibo, only the speculative evidential -*mein* imparts overtones of politeness when used in questions (Valenzuela 2003: 48–9). An example is in (145).

(145)   Mi-n-*mein*   e-a   nokon   wai   *Shipibo-Konibo*
        2-ERG-ASSUM   1-ABS   POSS1   garden:ABS
        oro-xon-ai?
        clear-BEN-INC
        'Would you please/perhaps clear my garden for me?'

In many languages of the world, markers of epistemic modalities and modal verbs make commands sound softer and less insistent (see examples in Aikhenvald 2010: 221). The use of the speculative evidential as a command-softener and exponent of politeness is consistent with its epistemic overtones of something one is not sure about, and is thus not insistent upon.

Evidentiality is not unique in having special meanings in non-declarative clause types. Numerous categories acquire additional meanings specific for imperative sentences and directive speech acts (see the discussion in Aikhenvald 2010: 89–113, on how imperatives are special). Politeness, or softening a command, is the most typical additional meaning for many forms and categories within directive speech acts. For instance, the 'velocity' suffix means 'quickly' in declarative clauses in Urarina, an isolate from Peru. In commands it indicates politeness and entreaty (Olawsky 2006: 471, 546–7, 571). In Yankunytjatjara, an Australian language, and also in Russian, the imperfective aspect in imperatives sounds politer than the perfective form, 'presumably because it implies less attention to the result or completion of the action in question' (Goddard 1983: 190).

Having politeness associated with evidential forms in commands – as illustrated in (142)–(143) – is consistent with the meanings and functions of commands as a sentence type. In (144) and (145), a question accompanied with an evidential appears to be used as a command strategy (not unlike imperatives as directives in many languages, including English: more on this in Aikhenvald 2010: 257–64). The overtones of politeness for the speculative evidential constitute an example of an extension specific for the context of a mild command or entreaty.

That evidentials may show additional meanings specific for the contexts of directive speech acts is independent of their dependencies on sentence types.

6.1.6 Evidentiality Depends on Polarity (Negation): Polarity > Evidentiality

There may be fewer evidentiality choices in negative clauses than in positive ones: that is, certain evidentiality contrasts may be neutralised in the negative forms. In Mỹky, an isolate from Brazilian Amazonia (Monserrat and Dixon 2003, Monserrat 2010: 57–9), no evidentials at all can be distinguished if the clause is negative. Structurally, this has to do with the fact that evidential markers (reported, inferred, and speculative) occupy the same slot in the verb word as does the negator. Fewer evidentiality distinctions are available in negative than in positive clauses in Kalmyk (Skribnik and Seesing 2014: 163).

A dependency between evidentiality and polarity may be realized in a tendency to use a particular evidential in negative clauses. Approximately 80% of negative clauses in the part of my Tariana corpus which reflects day-to-day activities and conversations contain the nonvisual evidential. (We can recall, from section 4.3, that the assumed and the reported evidential in the language are a feature of distinct genres of stories; and this frequency statement does not apply to them).

In the Luchuan dialect of Ryukyuan (Arakaki 2013: 159), the direct evidential is not used in nonpast tense in negative clauses; it is used in other tenses in both negative and positive clauses. This is an instance of a more complex dependency POLARITY/TENSE > EVIDENTIALITY.

6.1.7   Person/Number Depends on Evidentiality: Evidentiality > Person/Number

The choices available for person and number of the participant may depend on the choices made in the evidentiality system. In Estonian, three persons and two numbers are expressed if reported evidentiality is not specified. A selection is shown in (146).

(146)   mina   tule-n 'I come'   *Estonian*
        sina   tule-d 'you (sg) come'
        tema   tule-b 'he/she comes'
        meie   tule-me 'we come'

None of these person/number combinations are expressed in reported evidentiality, as shown in (147).

(147)   mina/sina/tema   tule-*vat*
        I/you/he/she/etc.   come-REPORTED
        'I/you/he/she etc. are reportedly coming'

Along similar lines, in Trio, a Carib language, the non-witnessed past form marked with a confix *ti-....-se* does not express person or number of the subject (Carlin 2004: 340–7). That is, the choice of non-witnessed past overrides the choice in person and number system. This dependency, EVIDENTIALITY > PERSON/NUMBER, has to do with evidential forms arising out of a nominalised (non-finite) form (see section 6.2).

An example of a dependency in the opposite direction, PERSON > EVIDENTIALITY, appears to come from Kashaya. Here the performative evidential is used only with first person. Its meaning is described as follows: 'speaker knows of what he speaks because he is performing the act himself or has just performed it' (Oswalt 1986: 34–42). Other evidentials (visual, auditory, inferential and quotative) are used with all persons. However, the interpretation of this instance depends on the status of the 'performative': based on its meaning, it can be treated as an exponent of access to knowledge and thus primarily belong to the domain of egophoricity rather than evidentiality.

⋯

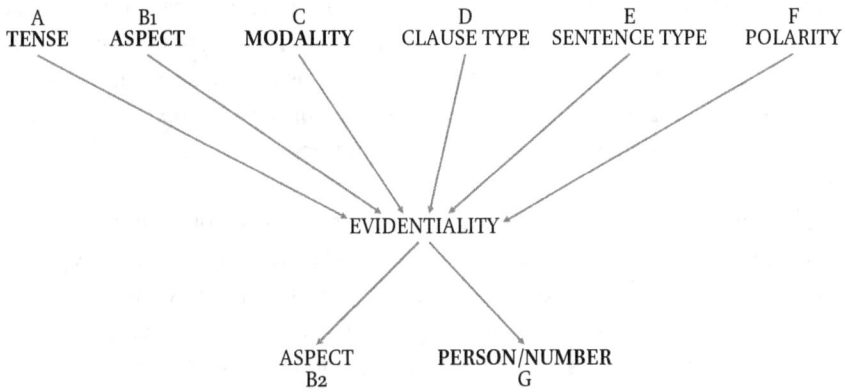

SCHEME 6   Evidentiality and its dependencies with other grammatical systems

The dependencies established here can be summarised as follows (the direction of the arrow reflects direction of a dependency). See Scheme 6.

That evidentiality should depend on polarity, or the contrast between a positive and negative clause, goes together with the general principle – that polarity, as a clausal category, is at the top of the hierarchy of grammatical categories (Aikhenvald and Dixon 2011: 197). The dependencies between evidentiality and clause type, and evidentiality and sentence type, can be accounted for by the fact that evidentiality which shows such correlations is a clause-based (or even a sentence-based) category. A number of further dependencies stem from a diachronic development of evidentials. This is what we turn to in section 6.2.

6.2   Diachronic Links between Evidentiality and Other Categories

Grammatical categories and grammatical forms may give rise to evidentials, as a consequence of their reanalysis and reinterpretation (see also Aikhenvald 2004: 271–87, Friedman 2018). The basis for this lies in the evidential extensions of non-evidential categories which may acquire meanings related to information source, and thus share similarities with evidentials. For instance, a conditional form may be used for non-firsthand information (this is what we saw in section 2).

6.2.1   From an Epistemic Modality and Future to an Evidential

Epistemic modalities may develop overtones of non-firsthand information (which is inherently uncertain), as does the conditional in French. They may then develop into non-firsthand evidentials. In Cree/Montagnais/Naskapi, an Algonquian language from Canada, conjunct dubitative forms have developed non-firsthand evidential meanings in contexts which prohibit the non-firsthand markers proper, for instance, under negation (see James, Clarke and MacKenzie 2001: 230; 254–7). This phenomenon is considered an innovation of Cree. Since the non-firsthand meaning 'has become conventionalised as a new meaning for dubitative suffixes in appropriate contexts', we hypothesise that an erstwhile evidential strategy is on its way towards becoming an evidential proper.

The development of a non-firsthand evidential may involve future, which – by its nature – is close to a non-indicative modality. A future clause typically includes an element of prediction concerning something unwitnessed and of subsequent lack of certainty. It can easily come to be associated with a description of events which the speaker has not witnessed personally, and which they can only talk about on the basis of an educated guess, an inference, an assumption, or hearsay. The non-firsthand evidential in Abkhaz and Circassian, two Northwest Caucasian languages, goes back to the future marker (Chirikba 2003: 262–4). The indirect evidential in Hill Patwin, *-boti/-beti* (Whistler 1986: 69–71) comes from a combination of the auxiliary *bo/be* 'be (locational)' followed by the definite future suffix. Along similar lines, two non-sensory markers with overtones of mirativity (one referring to expected information, and the other to unexpected facts) in Akha, a Tibeto-Burman language, developed from future markers: 'assumptive' future and 'speculative' future (Thurgood 1986: 221–2). According to Metslang and Pajusalu (2002: 101), the reported evidential marker *-na-* in South Estonian originates in the potential mood.

6.2.2 From a Perfect, Perfective, Resultative, or a Past Tense to an Evidential

A perfect, a resultative, a past tense and other forms with a completive meaning can acquire an additional overtone of inferred and generally of non-firsthand information. As Friedman (2003: 209) put it, both Balkan Slavic languages and Albanian developed evidential strategies using native past forms, and as the contextual variant meanings became invariant the strategies became grammaticalised. The non-firsthand evidential in Turkic, Iranian languages, and in many Finno-Ugric languages originates in anterior and perfect forms (Johanson 2003: 287 and further references in Aikhenvald 2004: 279–80). The non-firsthand evidential marker *-shapan* in Cree/Montagnais/Naskapi, goes back to a Proto-Algonquian perfect (James, Clarke and MacKenzie 2001: 247). Complex resultative constructions (involving perfective converbs and the copula 'be') gave rise to non-firsthand evidentials in Dargwa and Archi (Tatevosov 2001: 460–1; similar developments have been documented in other Nakh-Daghestanian languages, including Lezgi (see Greed 2017 and Forker 2018). Evidential extensions for the perfect form have been described for a number of Samoyedic languages, including Forest Enets (Skribnik and Kehayov 2018: 550).

The connection between perfect (or anterior) in its resultative meaning and a non-firsthand evidential is a typologically widespread tendency. The result of an action or state, or of an action or state viewed as relevant for the moment of speech is reinterpreted as having the meaning of inference based on visible traces, and other non-firsthand sources, such as assumption and hearsay. Once this range of non-firsthand meanings becomes the main meaning of the form, it can be considered an evidential.

There is some evidence for perfectives or resultatives giving rise to evidentials in larger systems. The Tuyuca nonvisual present marker may have evolved from an older perfect aspect construction (Malone 1988: 132). The emergence of the inferred evidential in Tariana involved the reanalysis of the anterior aspect marker *-nhi* accompanied by the visual evidential. Several past tenses may develop into different evidentials. In Kamaiurá, *je* 'reported' and *rak* 'attested' have clear cognates in past tense markers in other Tupí-Guaraní languages: the 'attested' evidential goes back to a recent past marker and the 'reported' to a remote past marker (Seki 2000: 344).

6.2.3   From a Nominalised Verb Form to an Evidential

Participles and other deverbal nominalizations are often used as evidentiality strategies, with the meaning of a non-firsthand or reported evidential. In Nenets (Perrot 1996, Skribnik and Kehayov 2018: 549–50) the non-firsthand forms come from de-subordinated nominalizations which include infinitives, participles and other denominal forms.[22] The non-firsthand past in Komi is based on a past participle (Leinonen 2000: 421). In Lithuanian, the reported evidentials developed out of active participles (Gronemeyer 1997: 93; see also Wälchli 2000 and Wiemer 2006). A similar path has been suggested by Overall (2014), for Aguaruna, a Jivaroan language, in the process of developing evidential distinctions. Nominalizations are used if the speaker had not witnessed what they are talking about. When used with first person, they may have the implications of reduced access to knowledge (along the lines of section 2.1, illustrated with examples (17) and (19), from Tariana). That is, something that had happened to the speaker that he was not aware of can be phrased using a nominalization. As Overall (2014: 240) puts it, in his discussion of example (148), 'the nominalised form is appropriate

---

22   The mechanisms of creating new verbal forms through de-subordination of dependent clauses and deverbal forms are addressed in Aikhenvald (2010: 275–80); see also Vallauri (2004), and papers in Yap et al. (2011).

because the speaker cannot be said to have witnessed his own birth (despite having been present!). The rest of the narrative is couched almost entirely in finite past tense forms, in keeping with the fact that the speaker witnessed all the events.'

(148)   mina   daa-hu-k   Pablo-i   *Aguaruna*
1SG.GEN   name-1sg-TOP   Pablo-COPULA.3DECL
wi-ka   akiina-u-ait-ha-i   comunidad
1sg-TOP   be.born.PERF.NOMIN-COPULA-1sg-DECL   community
Chikais
Chikais
'My name is Pablo. I was born in the community Chikais'

A similar path has been suggested for the development of evidential distinctions via reinterpretation of nominalizations (called participles) in Panare, a Carib language from Venezuela (Payne and Payne 2007: 349–50).

Nominalised speech complements are another frequent source for evidentials. The development of an evidentiality marker out of a complementation strategy involves 'de-subordination' of an erstwhile subordinate clause. That is, a complement clause of a verb of saying acquires the status of a main clause. Then, if the verb in such a dependent clause had a special form, this form takes on the status of a reported evidential. This scenario has been reconstructed for reported evidentials in Standard Estonian (see Harris and Campbell 1995: 99; and Wälchli 2000: 194–6 for further developments in Latvian). The original construction consisted of the main verb of speech or perception and an active participle in partitive form. Once the main verb is systematically omitted, what was a non-finite verb form occurs in a main clause. The only indication that the information comes from someone else is the present participle in partitive case. This form is now the reported evidential (illustrated in (140) and (141)). The nominalised forms (including participles) which gave rise to evidentials did not distinguish person or number of the participant in the first place. This historical path accounts for the lack of person – and number – distinctions in evidentials (see Scheme 6 on p. 99 here, and discussion in section 6.1.7), and the ensuing dependency.

⋯

Diachronic links can be used as an explanation for following recurrent interactions between evidentials and other grammatical categories, and also for the development of fused evidentiality:

1. The development path PAST TENSE/RESULTATIVE/PERFECT/PERFECTIVE > NON-FIRSTHAND EVIDENTIAL accounts for the mutual dependency between evidentials, aspect and tense.
2. The development path NON-INDICATIVE MODALITY > NON-FIRSTHAND EVIDENTIAL underlies the dependencies with modalities.

These dependencies for which a diachronic explanation is available are highlighted in Scheme 6 (p. 99 above).

6.3 Non-propositional Evidentials: Their Interactions with Other Grammatical Categories

Evidentials may have a non-propositional scope – that is, apply just to a noun phrase, as we saw in section 3.1.4. This is a feature they share with a number of other categories traditionally associated with a clause or its predicate, including tense, aspect, and modality.

In just a few languages, the same system of evidentials can apply to a noun phrase and to a clause. This is the case in Jarawara (example (58)), in a number of varieties of Latin American Spanish (examples (61)–(63)), and in Philippine languages (an example from Ilonggo is in (59)). The meanings of the evidential may differ depending on its scope. We can recall, from section 3.1.4, that in Ilonggo, a Philippine language, the reported evidential with NP scope may have epistemic overtones of doubt and uncertainty, in contrast to the same evidential with clausal scope. This is reminiscent of semantic differences in the shared temporal marking on noun phrases and on verbs in Halkomelem, a Salish language: temporal markers on verbs, with clausal scope, have exclusively a temporal meaning, while the same markers on noun phrases may have a temporal meaning (e.g. 'former spouse') or an additional, 'decessive' meaning (e.g. 'the late spouse') (Galloway 1993: 384, Wiltschko 2003: 682–90).

In a number of languages, a subset of propositional tense (and aspect) markers can be used with both clausal and noun phrase scope. This is what we find in Ashéninka Perené, an Arawak language from Peru (Mihas 2013: 24–7) and also in Baniwa of Içana (Ramirez 2001: 249, 340–2, 406). No similar examples of evidentials have been found in any language so far.

The marking and the meanings of non-propositional tense are often very different from that of propositional, or clausal, tense. Fewer tense meanings tend to be expressed on the non-propositional level (more on this in Bertinetto 2020, Aikhenvald 2021b on additional complexities in nominal tense and nominal aspect-cum-relevance in Tariana). Along similar lines, in the majority of instances semantic distinctions in non-propositional evidentials appear to involve access to a sensory information source – covering firsthand, or visual, information source.

Non-propositional evidential markers can be fused with deictics. In Lakondê, a Nambikwara language, noun phrases distinguish visual proximal and visual distant evidential forms (in opposition to evidentially unmarked, or neutral, forms). We can recall from section 3.1.4, p. 48, that a four-term evidentiality system with sentential scope is associated with verbs, and involves visual, dual visual, nonvisual and inferred (Eberhard 2018: 344–5).

In a few languages, information source is marked only at the NP level. These appear to always include a term with visual, or firsthand reference. The expression tends to be fused with another category.

Dyirbal, an Australian language (Dixon 2014), has a three-term system of noun markers which combine reference to visibility and spatial distance of the noun:
- *bala-* 'referent is visible and THERE' (that is, not near speaker);
- *yala-* 'referent is visible and HERE' (near speaker); and
- *ŋala-* 'referent is not visible'.

These distinctions are reminiscent of a cross-linguistically rather common evidential system, with a basic opposition between firsthand and non-firsthand information source (A1, Table 1). The non-visible marker covers something that is not seen but heard, or only known from its noise; something previously visible but now just audible; something neither visible nor audible; or something remembered from the past and not currently visible.

Somewhat more complex systems of non-propositional evidentiality whose scope is just the noun phrase have been described for Mataco-Mataguayan languages of Argentina and Paraguay. The markers combine reference to information source and to distance. Chorote distinguishes the following markers: 'visually perceived'; 'distant (or dead/consumed)'; 'not visible now but visible before'; 'invisible or unknown (used in myth)' (Carol 2011). The information-source markers in Maká, from the same family, cover the following meanings: 'close (can be reached by hand)'; 'close (cannot be reached by hand)'; 'far and visible; 'far and non-visible'; 'absent, seen before'; 'absent, never seen before' (Gerzenstein 1994: 166). Noun phrase evidentials in Nivaĉle (Gutiérrez 2015: 416) are fused with deictics, and distinguish firsthand versus non-firsthand information sources fused with presence versus absence at utterance time, with a special form for something formerly seen but no longer existent (see further discussion and a tentative reinterpretation in Jacques 2018: 118–19). No similar systems have so far been documented for evidentiality with clausal or sentential scope.

Santali (Munda: Neukom 2001: 42–4) has a special series of demonstrative pronouns referring to what is seen, or to what is heard. Both distinguish six degrees of distance combined with emphasis. The semantic extensions of these demonstratives are parallel to those in evidentiality systems: the visual demonstrative can refer to what is visible, while the auditive one may also refer to smell, taste and feeling (Neukom 2001: 42). (Note that a two-term audible versus inaudible demonstrative system has not been found in any language.)

None of these systems appear to display any dependencies between distance in space and the number of evidential distinctions expressed.

Evidential meanings are encoded within the case system in Tsou, a Formosan language (Pan 2018: 668, Yang 2000b). The expression of the visual evidential in nominative case is fused with distance. Tsou has two clausal cases, nominative and oblique, and a genitive case with just adnominal functions. There are four groups of evidential distinctions: visual, nonvisual, experiential, and non-experiential. Table 8 shows the case forms and their evidential meanings.

TABLE 8   Non-propositional evidentials and case markers in Tsou

	Nominative case	Oblique case	Genitive case
Visual	'e (near), si (intermediate), ta (remote)	ta	ta
Nonvisual	co	nca	–
Experiential	'o	to	to
Non-experiential	na	no	no

Distance is encoded just within the visual evidential in nominative case. This suggests a tentative dependency between case, the proximity of the entity to the speaker, and evidentiality. In (149), the roof is near the speaker and visible to them.

(149) a. mo   fhɨngoya   'e   sofɨ.   Tsou
          REAL.AV   red   NOM.VIS   roof
       'This roof (proximate to the speaker) is red.'

In (150), the roof is far from the speaker, and so the distal form of the visual evidential-cum-case is used.

(150) mo   fhɨngoya   ta   sofɨ.   Tsou
       REAL.AV   red   NOM.VIS   roof
       'That roof (distal to the speaker) is red.'

Example (151) illustrates the nonvisual evidential (nominative case): the speaker cannot see the child, but its cries can be heard.

(151) m-o   mongsi   co   oko
      AFFIX-REALIS cry(ACTOR.VOICE)   NOMINATIVE:NONVISUAL   child
      'The child is crying'

The genitive case stands apart from the clausal cases in that it does not have a nonvisual form. This suggests a tentative dependency between case and the number of evidential distinctions. The system of non-propositional evidentials is more complex than that with clausal or propositional scope: there we have just the distinction between reported evidential versus everything else.

Information source is fused with topicality in Maaka, a Chadic language (Storch and Coly 2014). As we can recall form section 4.2, noun phrase evidentials in Maaka encode visually acquired information, assumed information and information acquired through joint perception by the speaker and the addressee. In (104), the speaker has already seen the butterfly, to which the addressee's attention is directed. The butterfly from Mecca is marked with the visual evidential. This reflects the information source of the speaker. In (103), the child was seen by both the speaker and the addressee; the suffix -dìyà marks this joint perception. The nominal evidential -kà refers to speaker's assumption and intuition about an object (on which they have no firsthand information). In (152), the speaker talks about the addressee going to 'that very market' which is assumed to be taking place:

(152) ʔáa-kè-góm   *Maaka*
       CONDITIONAL-2sg:MASC-go
       gè-gòmà-à-*kà* (...)
       LOCATIVE-market-DEFINITE-ASSUMPTION
       'If you go to that very market (assumed to be taking place)....'

There are no interactions between clause types and the nominal assumption marker in Maaka. The assumption marker can be used in any clause type (including conditional, temporal, complement and other non-main clauses, and main clauses).

The two clausal evidentials in Maaka are the quotative *nà* and the reported *kònò*. An NP can be within the scope of the reported evidential. In contrast, an NP cannot be within the scope of a quotative – this is a major difference between the two. If the whole clause is within the scope of the reported evidential, it appears at the beginning of the clause, as in (153).

(153) kònò dóoshé mínéé-gòm ʔáshàakà   Maaka
REP tomorrow 1pl:FUT-go <NAME>
'Rumour has it that tomorrow we will go to the Ashaka cement factory'

If the evidential has an NP as its scope, it follows that NP, as in (154):

(154) sə~-ndée ʃà [líimó-wà]_NP kònò ʃà   Maaka
3sg:MASC-come:NARR WITH camel-DEF REP WITH
láà-n-tò
child-LINK-POSS:3sg:FEM
'He came with the reported camel and with its calf'

In (154), the information about the camel comes from speech report, or hearsay. In each case, the noun phrase marked with an evidential has to be definite and also the topic.

The Southern Nambikwara dialect complex has a remarkably complex set of nominal tense markers fused with information source. The meanings expressed are observational, inferential and quotative. Nouns are also specified for whether they are definite, or not, and represent given or new information (raised numbers stand for tones). Examples for wa^3lin^3-su^3-a^2 (manioc-CL:BONE.LIKE-DEF) 'the manioc root' (Lowe 1999: 282–3) are in (155)–(156). In (155), the marker 'definite and current' implies visual information source for the manioc root. The evidential in (155) indicates dual perspective – that of the speaker and of the addressee. The evidential in (156) indicates the information source of just the speaker.

(155) wa^3lin^3-su^3-ai^2na^2 Southern Nambikwara
manioc-CLASSIFIER:BONE.LIKE-DEFINITE.CURRENT
'This manioc root which we see both before us now'

(156) wa^3lin^3-su^3-$nũ^1.tã^2$ Southern Nambikwara
manioc-CLASSIFIER:BONE.LIKE-INFERENTIAL.DEFINITE.
UNMARKED
'The manioc root that must have been at some time past, as inferred by me (but not by you)'

TABLE 9   Nominal evidentials and tense markers in Southern Nambikwara

-a^2	definite, unmarked
-ai^2na^2	definite, current
-in^3ti^2	observational, recent past, given
-$ait^3ta^3li^2$	observational, mid past, given
-$ait^3tã^2$	observational, mid past, new
-$ait^3tã^2$	definite, remote past, new
-$nũ^1tã^2$	inferential, definite, unmarked
-$nũ^1tai^2na^2$	inferential, current
-$au^3teʔ^1tã^2$	quotative, mid past, given

The verbal categories of tense, aspect, evidentiality and given information are different, in form and in meaning (Lowe 1999: 275, Eberhard 2018: 340). The meanings expressed include visual, inferred, reported and general knowledge (with further distinctions depending on whether the information is available to just the speaker, or the speaker and the addressee) – see Table 5.

Table 9 contains a list of attested nominal suffixes in Southern Nambikwara which combine the information on evidentiality, nominal tense, definiteness of the entity and its newness versus 'givenness' (Lowe 1999: 282).

The set of markers appears to show some gaps which could be indicative of potential dependencies between evidentiality, tense, and definiteness on nouns. For instance, 'observational' evidentiality seems to exclude 'current', which implies 'at the time and place reached in the discourse'. This is reminiscent of the lack of present tense forms in inferred evidentials in some languages (such as Tariana and Tucano, but curiously enough, neither in Southern Nambikwara nor Mamaindê: Tables 4–5 above).

Southern Nambikwara and Maaka are the only languages we know which involve information sharing in their non-propositional evidential marking. In contrast to Maaka, nominal tense and evidentiality are combined in the Southern Nambikwara suffixes. Non-propositional evidentials in both languages interrelate with topicality of the noun. However, both systems appear to be unique. More examples are needed, before we can proceed to make any typological generalizations.

6.4   Evidentials and Other Grammatical Categories: A Summary

Evidentials interact with tense, aspect, sentence types (or mood system), polarity, clause types, modality and person and number. Dependencies between tense, aspect, modality, person-number (see Scheme 6) and evidentiality can be partly explained by their historical pathways.

Evidentials may acquire additional meanings, not directly related to information source. They may have epistemic meanings, and also have further values as tokens of person. This may create a further basis for development of dependencies between evidentiality, person systems and modality. We have seen that evidentials can acquire overtones of uncontrolled action, deferred realization and 'surprise', especially in the context of first person. When used in commands, a reported evidential may have overtones of politeness: it makes a command sound less direct, allowing a speaker to distance themselves from a potentially threatening direct order. That is, clausal evidentials may have an effect of establishing cognitive distance.

Perceptual meanings and meanings of information source can be expressed just within a noun phrase. They then interrelate with noun phrase categories – including physical distance in space (especially in demonstrative systems), pragmatic status and grammatical function (shown by case). However, due to the comparative rarity of non-propositional evidentiality, few if any dependencies between these and other categories can be established at our present stage of knowledge.

The synchronic relationship between evidentiality and the notion of distance in space may be explained diachronically. In a number of languages (including Wintu, Sissala and Lega) clausal evidentials have been shown to have come from demonstratives (see Aikhenvald 2021a). This alerts us to further links evidentials may have, and a possible further connection between clausal and non-propositional evidentiality as a matter for future investigation.

The actual use of an evidential may depend on speaker's intention, and information structure. In !Xun, firsthand and non-firsthand evidentials are optional and are only used if the speaker wants to focus on the information source (König 2013). In Turkic languages, focus in discourse is associated with the use of the non-firsthand evidential (Johanson 2003). In Trio, the non-witnessed past is associated with the category of theticity whereby an event is taken as a whole (Carlin 2004: 247; 2011). In Abkhaz, an aside remark can be cast in the non-firsthand evidential (with the story told using evidentially neutral forms) (Chirikba 2003: 247–8; and further examples in Aikhenvald 2004: 317–18). In view of this, a correlation between topicality of a noun, or a noun phrase, and the use of evidentials attested in Maaka and in Southern Nambikwara should not come as a surprise. But given the rarity of such systems, this remains a typological curio – for now.

7 What Can We Conclude?

The four ways of expressing knowledge through grammar – evidentiality, egophoricity, mirativity, and epistemic modality – interact. Some can develop overtones of the others. We have seen examples of evidentials having egophoric, epistemic, and mirative overtones. Markers of epistemic modality and egophoricity may acquire additional meanings involving information sources (section 2).

Evidentials stand apart from other means of expressing knowledge in
(a) their scope,
(b) the possibility of double marking,
(c) the time reference different from that of the predicate,
(d) the option of being negated or questioned separately from the predicate of the clause, and € specific correlations with speech genres and social environment.

The presence of grammatical evidentials in Amazonian languages correlates with the cultural requirement of being precise in stating one's information source. The correct use of evidential defines a person as a reliable member of the community. And the patterns of evidential use change with the advent of new means of acquiring information (see section 3, and Table 3).

Evidentials can be semantically complex. They may combine reference to the information source of the speaker and of the addressee, and access to information source. The general knowledge evidential has been identified as a separate term in Yongning Na, a Tibeto-Burman language, in Kalmyk and Buryat (Mongolic languages), and in Mamaindê and Southern Nambikwara, the two extant languages from the Nambikwara family in Brazil. Southern Nambikwara, Conchucos Quechua and Sihas Quechua distinguish mutual versus individual access to information source within their evidential systems. However, in contrast to the two Quechua languages, Southern Nambikwara extends this distinction to reported evidentials (section 4.2, and Table 3).

The uses of evidentials often correlate with discourse genres and can be considered tokens of genres – this is what we saw in section 4.3. In many languages – including Mparntwe Arrernte, Ersu, Tariana and many more – the reported evidential is used in narratives. There may be multiple motivations for the use of an evidential: what one can see can be interpreted as a fact, generally accessible by vision. What one cannot see (a supernatural activity or a spirit's doings) may always be cast in a nonvisual evidential. A nonvisual evidential may be used to describe one's own feelings and internal states, and also that of the people close to the speaker.

Alternatively, a term within an evidential system may reflect access to knowledge and knowledge sharing, thus overlapping with the domain of egophoricity. The assumed evidential in Tariana is a case in point (section 4.3). As a feature of traditional story genres – part of Tariana heritage and lore – the evidential term suffers partial obsolescence, as there are fewer and fewer elders left to authoritatively share ancestral knowledge.

Evidentials and epistemic modalities have an unequal relationship. In numerous instances across the world, evidentials stem from reinterpretation of epistemic markers. Developments in the opposite direction are few. An obsolescent language with evidentiality may reinterpret the erstwhile markers of information source as modals, as it succumbs to the pressure of a dominant language with no evidentials. Alternatively, an attempt to express one's information source in an ethnolect of a dominant language with no grammatical evidentials may involve a modal verb. This is similar to the way in which speakers of languages with evidentials resort to modals in their attempt to render these meanings into languages such as English. The proper meaning of information sources is lost in translation, and epistemic modals step in as poor substitutes (section 5). Evidentials show a set of dependencies with other grammatical categories. Some of these can be explained through their origins and development (section 6).

Each of the four groups of grammatical means for expressing knowledge have their specific features. Each is responsible for shaping successful communication and interpersonal relationships. Evidentials have a special place within the web of knowledge-related forms: this is where the grammar of a language and the social world of its speakers come together.

Appendix: Knowledge through Grammar: Further Categories, Further Options

Knowledge-related categories extend beyond the four groups outlined in section 1 above. One of these is reality status, or the distinction between realis and irrealis. Realis refers to 'something which has happened or is happening and may be extended to refer to something which is certain to happen'. Irrealis 'refers to something which has not (yet) happened; often also used for something which did not happen in the past, but might have' (see Dixon 2012: 22–25). Irrealis can be considered another way of expressing epistemic meanings – to do with treating information as reliable, possible, probable and so on. Depending on the language, epistemic modalities may be realised within irrealis. Or they can be expressed independently. Confusing epistemic modalities with reality status obliterates the differences between independent categories in many languages (see, for instance, by Ziegeler 2011). As shown in Aikhenvald (2004: 108–9), the meanings of irrealis may overlap with those of unwitnessed evidentials as a semantic extension. In contrast, information concerning interactions between reality status, mirativity, and egophoricity is extremely scarce. In order to keep this contribution to a reasonable length, I have chosen not to include reality status in this discussion.

A further issue concerns the exact content of 'access to information'. This may include:

(i) representation of knowledge as available, or unavailable, to the speaker, and representation of knowledge as personal versus not personal, reflecting 'privileged access' to knowledge;
(ii) whether or not information is shared by speaker, addressee, and others.

According to Watters (ms), 'representation of knowledge' (sense (i)) and 'access to knowledge', or 'knowledge sharing' (sense (ii)), acquire independent expression in Dzongkha. This opens up the option of further splitting up the grammatical realization of the complex of meanings subsumed under 'access to knowledge'.

Further topics which may well be relevant include speaker's perspective, 'intersubjectivity', and empathy (in many languages expressed through optional particles). How they fit into the grammatical expression of knowledge is a matter for further studies.

Furthermore, meanings associated with each of the groups of categories I–IV can be expressed in ways additional to the dedicated grammatical categories. Epistemic modal meanings can be expressed via adverbs, parentheticals, or even gestures. The same for mirative meanings (DeLancey 2001 offers a discussion of interjections indicating surprise as an analogy to mirative marking in grammar). Expression of access to information (or egophoric meanings) through means other than verbal morphology is a matter for further study. In many languages, these meanings appear to be expressed through discourse particles and adverbs. The locus of marking for each of the four groups of categories is a language-specific matter which we leave for now.

Commentary

Many of the issues concerning evidentiality, including previous studies of the subject and comprehensive illustration of various types of evidential systems, are discussed in fair detail in the following books which I published or edited, and also papers:

Aikhenvald, Alexandra Y. 2003. 'Evidentiality in typological perspective', pp. 1–31 of *Studies in evidentiality*, edited by Alexandra Y. Aikhenvald and R. M. W. Dixon. Amsterdam: John Benjamins (written in 2000 and circulated before publication).

Aikhenvald, Alexandra Y. 2004. *Evidentiality*. Oxford: Oxford University Pres.

Aikhenvald, Alexandra Y. 2014. 'The grammar of knowledge in typological perspective', pp. 1–51 of *The grammar of knowledge: a cross-linguistic typology*, edited by Alexandra Y. Aikhenvald and R. M. W. Dixon. Oxford: Oxford University Press.

Aikhenvald, Alexandra Y. 2015. 'Evidentiality and its interrelations with other categories'. *Linguistic Typology* 19: 239–77.

Aikhenvald, Alexandra Y. 2015. *The languages of the Amazon*. Oxford: Oxford University Press (especially Chapter 9 'How to know things: evidentials in Amazonia').

Aikhenvald, Alexandra Y. 2018. Editor of *The Oxford Handbook of evidentiality*. Oxford: Oxford University Press, and especially Chapter 1 'Evidentiality: the framework', pp. 1–46.

A comprehensive bibliography is at Oxford Bibliography Online: Evidentials (Aikhenvald 2015c). This is an updateable resource with summaries and evaluation for each entry (last updated 2015). A description of what evidentiality is like and what it is good for is in my short book for general audience *I saw the dog: how language works* (London: Profile books, 2021).

This essay, like all my previous work on evidentiality, is based on a thorough examination of several hundred grammars of languages with and without evidentiality (expanding on the original database used for Aikhenvald 2004). Tariana examples stem from my original fieldwork (with the corpus consisting of approximately 35 hours of recording, and growing).

References

Adelaar, Willem F. H. 1977. *Tarma Quechua: Grammar, Texts, Dictionary*. Lisse: De Ridder.

Adelaar, Willem F. H. 2013. 'A Quechuan mirative?', pp. 95–110 of *Linguistic expression of perception and cognition*, edited by Alexandra Y. Aikhenvald and Anne Storch. Leiden: Brill.

Adelaar, Willem F. H. 2017. 'A typological overview of Aymaran and Quechuan language structure', pp. 651–82 of *The Cambridge Handbook of linguistic typology*, edited by Alexandra Y. Aikhenvald and R. M. W. Dixon. Cambridge: Cambridge University Press.

Aikhenvald, Alexandra Y. 2002. *Language contact in Amazonia*. Oxford: Oxford University Press.
Aikhenvald, Alexandra Y. 2003a. *A grammar of Tariana*. Cambridge: Cambridge University Press.
Aikhenvald, Alexandra Y. 2003b. 'Evidentiality in typological perspective', pp. 1–31 of *Studies in evidentiality*, edited by Alexandra Y. Aikhenvald and R. M. W. Dixon. Amsterdam: John Benjamins.
Aikhenvald, Alexandra Y. 2004. *Evidentiality*. Oxford: Oxford University Press.
Aikhenvald, Alexandra Y. 2008. 'Multilingual imperatives: the elaboration of a category in north-west Amazonia'. *International Journal of American Linguistics* 74: 189–225.
Aikhenvald, Alexandra Y. 2010. *Imperatives and commands*. Oxford: Oxford University Press.
Aikhenvald, Alexandra Y. 2011. 'Speech reports: A cross-linguistic perspective', pp. 290–326 of *Language at large. Essays on syntax and semantics*, by Alexandra Y. Aikhenvald and R. M. W. Dixon. Leiden: Brill.
Aikhenvald, Alexandra Y. 2012. 'The essence of mirativity'. *Linguistic Typology* 16: 435–85.
Aikhenvald, Alexandra Y. 2013. 'The language of value and the value of language'. *Hau: a journal of ethnographic theory* 3 (2): 55–73.
Aikhenvald, Alexandra Y. 2014. 'The grammar of knowledge in typological perspective', pp. 1–51 of *The grammar of knowledge*, edited by Alexandra Y. Aikhenvald and R. M. W. Dixon. Oxford: Oxford University Press.
Aikhenvald, Alexandra Y. 2015a. 'Evidentiality and its interrelations with other categories'. *Linguistic Typology* 19: 239–77.
Aikhenvald, Alexandra Y. 2015b. *The languages of the Amazon*. Oxford: Oxford University Press.
Aikhenvald, Alexandra Y. 2015c. 'Evidentiality: a bibliography'. *Oxford Bibliographies in Linguistics*, ed. Mark Aronoff. New York: Oxford University Press.
Aikhenvald, Alexandra Y. 2015d. 'Distance, direction, and relevance: How to choose and use a demonstrative in Manambu'. *Anthropological Linguistics* 57:1, 1–45.
Aikhenvald, Alexandra Y. 2016. *How gender shapes the world*. Oxford: Oxford University Press.
Aikhenvald, Alexandra Y. 2018a. 'Evidentiality: the framework', pp. 1–46 of Aikhenvald (ed.).
Aikhenvald, Alexandra Y. 2018b. 'Evidentiality and language contact', pp. 148–72 of Aikhenvald (ed.).
Aikhenvald, Alexandra Y. 2018. Editor of *The Oxford Handbook of evidentiality*. Oxford: Oxford University Press.
Aikhenvald, Alexandra Y. 2019. 'Tenets of the unseen: the preferred information source for the supernatural in Tariana'. *Mouth* 4: 59–75 (special issue *Taboo in language and discourse*, edited by Alexandra Y. Aikhenvald and Anne Storch).

Aikhenvald, Alexandra Y. 2020. 'Language loss and language gain in Amazonia: on newly emergent varieties of a national language', pp. 7–34 of *Amazonian Spanish. Language contact and evolution*, edited by Stefan Fafulas. Amsterdam: John Benjamins.

Aikhenvald, Alexandra Y. 2021a. 'The grammaticalization of evidentiality', pp. 602–10 of *The Oxford Handbook of Grammaticalization*, edited by Heiko Narrog and Bernd Heine. Oxford: Oxford University Press.

Aikhenvald, Alexandra Y. 2021b. 'Beyond nominal tense: temporality, aspect, and relevance in Tariana noun phrases'. *Studies in Language*. https//doi.org/10.1075/sl20056.aik.

Aikhenvald, Alexandra Y. 2021c. 'The ways of speaking and the means of knowing: the Tariana of northwest Amazonia'. To appear in *The integration of language and society: a cross-linguistic typology*, edited by Alexandra Y. Aikhenvald, R. M. W. Dixon, and Nerida Jarkey. Oxford: Oxford University Press.

Aikhenvald, Alexandra Y. and R. M. W. Dixon. 2003. Editors of *Studies in evidentiality*. Amsterdam: John Benjamins.

Aikhenvald, Alexandra Y. and R. M. W. Dixon. 2011. 'Dependencies between grammatical systems', pp. 170–204 of *Language at large. Essays on syntax and semantics*, by Alexandra Y. Aikhenvald and R. M. W. Dixon. Leiden: Brill. (originally published in *Language* 74. 56–80, 1998).

Aikhenvald, Alexandra Y. and R. M. W. Dixon. 2014. Editors of *The grammar of knowledge: a cross-linguistic typology*. Oxford: Oxford University Press.

Aikhenvald, Alexandra Y., R. M. W. Dixon, and Nerida Jarkey. 2021. Forthcoming. 'The integration of language and society: a cross-linguistic perspective'. To appear in *The integration of language and society*, edited by Alexandra Y. Aikhenvald, R. M. W. Dixon, and Nerida Jarkey. Oxford: Oxford University Press.

Aksu-Koç, A. A. and D. I. Slobin. 1986. 'A psychological account of the development and use of evidentials in Turkish', pp. 159–67 of Chafe and Nichols (eds.).

Alcázar, Asier. 2018. 'Dizque and other emergent evidential forms in Romance languages', pp. 725–740 of Aikhenvald (ed.).

Arakaki, Tomoko. 2013. *Evidentials in Ryukyuan: the Shuri Dialect of Luchuan*. Leiden: Brill.

Bai, Junwei. 2020. 'A grammar of Munya'. PhD thesis, James Cook University.

Baraby, Anne-Marie. 2017. 'Imperatives and evidentiality in Innu', pp. 53–77 of *Imperatives and directives strategies*, edited by D. Van Olmen and S. Heinold. Amsterdam: John Benjamins.

Barnes, Janet. 1984. 'Evidentials in the Tuyuca verb'. *International Journal of American Linguistics* 50: 255–271.

Bergqvist, Henrik. 2017. 'The role of perspective in epistemic marking'. *Lingua* 186: 5–20.

Bertinetto, Pier Marco. 2013. 'Ayoreo (Zamuco) as a radical tenseless language'. *Quaderni del Laboratorio di Linguistica* 12: 1–16.

Bertinetto, Pier Marco. 2020. 'On non-propositional tense'. *Linguistic Typology* 24: 311–52.

Boas, Frans. 1938. 'Language', pp. 124–45 of *General Anthropology*, by Franz Boas. Boston, New York: D. C. Heath and Company.

Boas, Frans. 1942. 'Language and culture', pp. 178–84 of *Studies in the history of culture: the disciplines of the humanities*, by Franz Boas. Menasha: The George Banta Publishing Co.

Brosig, Benjamin and Elena Skribnik. 2018. 'Evidentiality in Mongolic', pp. 554–79 of Aikhenvald (ed.).

Brown, P. and S. C. Levinson. 1987. *Politeness. Some universals in language usage*. Cambridge: Cambridge University Press.

Bullock, A. and O. Stallybrass. 1988. *The Fontana dictionary of modern thought*. London: Fontana/Collins.

Bunte, P. A. and M. B. Kendall 1981. 'When is an error not an error? Notes on language contact and the question of interference.' *Anthropological Linguistics* 23: 1–7.

Carlin, Eithne B. 2004. *A Grammar of Trio, a Cariban Language of Suriname*. Frankfurt: Peter Lang.

Carlin, Eithne B. 2018. 'Evidentiality and the Cariban languages', pp. 315–323 of Aikhenvald (ed.).

Carol, Javier J. 2011. 'Determinantes demostrativos en chorote (mataguayo). Interrelación con la modalidad, la temporalidad y la evidencialidad'. *Indiana* 28: 227–54.

Chafe, Wallace L. 1986. 'Evidentiality in English Conversation and Academic Writing,' pp. 261–72 of Chafe and Nichols (eds.).

Chafe, Wallace and Johanna Nichols (eds.). 1986. *Evidentiality: The linguistic coding of epistemology*. Norwood, NJ: Ablex.

Chang, Henry. 2015. 'Nominal tense in Tsou: *Nia* and its syntax/semantics'. *UCLA Working Papers in Linguistics* 17: 57–68.

Chirikba, V. 2003. 'Evidential category and evidential strategy in Abkhaz,' pp. 243–72 of Aikhenvald and Dixon (eds.).

Chung, Sandra and Alan Timberlake 1985. 'Tense, aspect and mood', pp. 202–58 of *Language Typology and Syntactic Description*. Volume III. *Grammatical categories and the lexicon*, edited by T. Shopen. Cambridge: Cambridge University Press.

Comrie, Bernard. 1976. *Aspect*. Cambridge: Cambridge University Press.

Curnow, Timothy Jowan. 2002. 'Types of interaction between evidentials and first-person subjects'. *Anthropological Linguistics* 44: 178–96.

Daguman, Josephine. 2018. 'The reportative in the languages of the Philippines', pp. 674–692 of Aikhenvald (ed.).

De Haan, Ferdinand. 2013. 'Coding of Evidentiality', chapter 78 of *The World Atlas of Language Structures Online*, edited by Matthew S. Dryer and Martin Haspelmath. Leipzig: Max Planck Institute for Evolutionary Anthropology.

DeLancey, Scott. 1986. 'Evidentiality and volitionality in Tibetan', pp. 203–13 of Chafe and Nichols (eds.).

DeLancey, Scott. 1997. 'Mirativity: The grammatical marking of unexpected information'. *Linguistic Typology* 1: 33–52.

DeLancey, Scott. 2001. 'The mirative and evidentiality.' *Journal of Pragmatics* 33: 359–367.

DeLancey, Scott. 2003. 'Lhasa Tibetan', pp. 270–88 of *The Sino-Tibetan languages*, edited by Graham Thurgood, G. and Randy J. LaPolla. London: Routledge.

DeLancey, Scott. 2012. 'Still mirative after all these years'. *Linguistic Typology* 16: 529–564.

DeLancey, Scott. 2018. 'Evidentiality in Tibetic', pp. 580–594 of Aikhenvald (ed.).

Dendale, Patrick. 1993. 'Le conditionnel de l'information incertaine: marqueur modal ou marqueur évidentiel?', pp. 165–76 of *Proceedings of the XXe Congrès International de Linguistique et Philologie Romanes, Tome I, Section I. La phrase*, edited by Gerold Hilty. Tübingen: Francke.

Dickinson, Connie. 2000. 'Mirativity in Tsafiki'. *Studies in Language* 24: 379–421.

Dixon, R. M. W. 2003. 'Evidentiality in Jarawara', pp. 165–188 of Aikhenvald and Dixon (eds.).

Dixon, R. M. W. 2004. *The Jarawara Language of Southern Amazonia*. Oxford: Oxford University Press.

Dixon, R. M. W. 2010a. *Basic Linguistic Theory*. Volume 1. *Methodology*. Oxford: Oxford University Press.

Dixon, R. M. W. 2010b. *Basic Linguistic Theory*. Volume 2. *Grammatical topics*. Oxford: Oxford University Press.

Dixon, R. M. W. 2012. *Basic Linguistic Theory*. Volume 3. *Further grammatical topics*. Oxford: Oxford University Press.

Dixon, R. M. W. 2014. 'The non-visible marker in Dyirbal', pp. 171–89 of Aikhenvald and Dixon (eds.).

Dixon, R. M. W. 2016. *Are some languages better than others?* Oxford: Oxford University Press.

Dixon, R. M. W. 2021. *The essence of linguistic analysis: an integrated approach*. Leiden: Brill.

Doble, Marion. 1987. 'A description of some aspects of Ekari language structure'. *Oceanic Linguistics* 26: 55–113.

Dozon, A. 1879. *Manuel de la langue chkipe ou albanaise*. Paris: Ernest Leroux.

Eberhard, David M. 2009. *A grammar of Mamaindê: a Northern Nambikwara language and its cultural context*. Amsterdam: LOT.

Eberhard, David M. 2012. 'The Mamaindê Tense/Evidentiality System'. *Word Structure* 5: 129–164.

Eberhard, David M. 2018. 'Evidentiality in Nambikwara languages', pp. 333–56 of Aikhenvald (ed.).

Egerod, S. 1985. 'Typological features in Akha', pp. 96–104 of *Linguistics of the Sino-Tibetan area: the state of the art (Papers presented to Paul K. Benedict for his 71st birthday)*, edited by Graham Thurgood, James A. Matisoff, and David Bradley. Canberra: Pacific Linguistics.

Faller, Martina. 2002. 'Semantics and pragmatics of evidentials in Cuzco Quechua'. PhD, Stanford University.

Fleck, David. 2007. 'Evidentiality and double tense in Matses.' *Language* 83: 589–614.

Floyd, Rick. 1996. 'The Radial Structure of the Wanka Reportative', pp. 895–941 of *Cognitive linguistics in the redwoods: the expansion of a new paradigm in linguistics*, edited by Eugene Casad. Berlin: Mouton De Gruyter.

Floyd, Rick. 1999. *The structure of evidential categories in Wanka Quechua*. Summer Institute of Linguistics and University of Texas, Arlington.

Floyd, Simeon. 2005. 'The poetics of evidentiality in South American storytelling'. *Santa Barbara Papers in Linguistics* 16: 28–41.

Forker, Diana. 2013. *A grammar of Hinuq*. Berlin: De Gruyter.

Forker, Diana. 2014. 'The grammar of knowledge in Hinuq', pp. 52–58 of Aikhenvald and Dixon (eds.).

Forker, Diana. 2018. 'Evidentiality in Nakh-Daghestanian languages', pp. 49–509 of Aikhenvald (ed.).

Frajzyngier, Zygmunt. 1985. 'Truth and the Indicative Sentence.' *Studies in Language* 9: 243–54.

Friedman, Victor. 1986. 'Evidentiality in the Balkans: Bulgarian, Macedonian and Albanian', pp. 168–87 of Chafe and Nichols (eds.).

Friedman, Victor. 2003. 'Evidentiality in the Balkans with special attention to Macedonian and Albanian', pp. 189–218 of *Studies in evidentiality*, edited by Alexandra Y. Aikhenvald and R. M. W. Dixon. Amsterdam: John Benjamins.

Friedman, Victor. 2010. 'The age of the Albanian admirative: a problem in historical semantics', pp. 31–9 of *Ex Anatolia Lux. Anatolian and Indo-European studies in honor of H. Craig Melchert on the occasion of his sixty-fifth birthday*, edited by Ronald Kim, Norbert Oettinger, Elisabeth Rieken, and Michael Weiss. Ann Arbor: Beech Stave Press, 31–9.

Friedman, Victor. 2012. 'Perhaps Mirativity is Phlogiston, but Admirativity is Perfect: On Balkan Evidential Strategies'. *Linguistic Typology* 16: 505–527.

Friedman, Victor. 2018. 'Where do evidentials come from?', pp. 124–47 of Aikhenvald (ed.).

Furbee, N. Louanna. 2006. 'Language and the religion of politics in Chiapas', pp. 189–204 of *Language, culture and the individual. A tribute to Paul Friedrich*, edited by Catherine O'Neil, Mary Scoggin & Kevin Tuite. Munich: Lincom Europa.

Galloway, Brent D. 1993. *A grammar of Upriver Halkomelem*. Berkeley: University of California Press.

García Salido, Gabriela. 2014a. 'Así cuentan los tepehuanos: el uso y función del reportativo en el discurso o'dam'. *Revista de Historia de la Universidad Juárez del Estado de Durango*. Instituto de Investigaciones Históricas: 6:19–31.

García Salido, Gabriela. 2014b. 'Clause Linkage in Southeastern Tepehuan, a Uto-Aztecan Language of Northern Mexico'. PhD dissertation, University of Texas-Austin.

Gerzenstein, Anna. 1994. *Lengua maká: Estudio descriptivo*. Archivo de Lenguas Indoamericanas. Buenos Aires: Universidad de Buenos Aires, Facultad de Filosofia y Letras, Instituto de Lingüística.

Gipper, Sonja. 2014. 'Intersubjective evidentials in Yurakaré. Evidence from conversational data and a first step toward a comparative perspective'. *Studies in Language* 38: 792–835.

Goddard, C. 1983. 'A semantically-oriented grammar of the Yankunytjatjara dialect of the Western Desert language'. PhD dissertation, Australian National University.

Gomez-Imbert, Elsa. 2014. 'Evidentials and other verbal categories in Tatuyo and Barasana (Eastern Tukanoan)'. Paper presented at a Workshop Evidentiality in interaction with other linguistic categories, University of Leiden, 21 February 2014.

Greed, Teija. 2014. 'The expression of knowledge in Tatar', pp. 69–88 of Aikhenvald and Dixon (eds.).

Greed, Teija. 2017. 'Evidential coding in Lezgi'. *Languages of the Caucasus* 2: 1–33.

Greed, Teija. 2018a. 'From perfect to narrative tense: The development of an evidential meaning examined generally and in the Even language'. *Studies in Language* 42: 923–66.

Greed, Teija. 2018b. 'The quotative in Bashkir'. *Studia Orientalia Electronica* 6: 23–55.

Gronemeyer, C. 1997. Evidentiality in Lithuanian. *Working Papers* 46. 93–112, Lund University, Department of Linguistics.

Grosh, Sylvia and Andrew Grosh. 2004. *Grammar essentials for the Kaluli language*. Ms. Ukarumpa: Summer Institute of Linguistics.

Gruzdeva, E. Ju. 2001. 'Imperative sentences in Nivkh', pp. 59–77 of *Typology of imperative constructions*, edited by V. S. Xrakovskij. Munich: Lincom Europa.

Grzech, Karolina. 2016. 'The non-evidential meaning of the Tena Kichwa "direct evidential"'. *York Papers in Linguistics* 3: 73–94.

Guillaume, Antoine. 2008. *A grammar of Cavineña*. Berlin: Mouton de Gruyter.

Gutiérrez, Analía. 2015. 'Evidential determiners in Nivaĉle'. *Anthropological Linguistics* 57: 412–443.

Hansson, I-L. 1994. 'The interplay between the verb particle 'ə' and the sentence particles in Akha.' Paper presented at the 27th International Conference on Sino-Tibetan Languages and Linguistics. Paris, 12–16 October.

Hansson, I-L. 2003. 'Akha', pp. 236–52. *The Sino-Tibetan languages*, edited by Graham Thurgood and Randy J. LaPolla. London: Routledge.

Hardman, M. J. 1986. 'Data-source marking in the Jaqi languages', pp. 113–36 of Chafe and Nichols (eds.).

Hargreaves, David. 2018. '"Am I blue?": Privileged access constraints in Kathmandu Newar', pp. 79–107 of *Egophoricity*, edited by Simeon Floyd, Elisabeth Norcliffe and Lila San Roque. Amsterdam: John Benjamins.

Harris, Alice C. and Lyle Campbell. 1995. *Historical Syntax in Cross-linguistic Perspective*. Cambridge: Cambridge University Press.

Haspelmath, Martin. 1993. *A grammar of Lezgian*. Berlin: Mouton De Gruyter.

Hein, Veronika. 2007. 'The mirative and its interplay with evidentiality in the Tibetan dialect of Tabo (Spiti)'. *Linguistics of the Tibeto-Burman Area* 30: 195–214.

Heine, Bernd and Heiko Narrog. 2020. Editors of *Grammaticalization from a Typological Perspective*. Oxford: Oxford University Press.

Heine, Bernd and Heiko Narrog. 2021. Editors of *The Oxford Handbook of Grammaticalization*, second edition. Oxford: Oxford University Press.

Hill, Jane H. 2005. *A grammar of Cupeño*. University of California Publications in Linguistics 136.

Hill, Jane H. and J. T. Irvine. 1992. 'Introduction', pp. 1–23 of *Responsibility and evidence in oral discourse*, edited by Jane H. Hill and Judith T. Irvine. Cambridge: Cambridge University Press.

Hill, Nathan W. 2012. '"Mirativity" does not exist: *h7dug* in "Lhasa" Tibetan and other suspects'. *Linguistic Typology* 16: 389–433.

Hill, Nathan W. and Gawne, L. 2017. 'The contribution of Tibetan languages to the study of evidentiality', pp. 1–38 of *Evidential Systems of Tibetan Languages*, edited by L. Gawne & Nathan W. Hill. Berlin: Mouton De Gruyter.

Hintz, Daniel J. 2014. 'South Conchucos Quechua', pp. 463–81 of *How languages work. An introduction to language and linguistics*, edited by Carol Genetti. Cambridge: Cambridge University Press.

Hintz, Daniel J. and Diane M. Hintz. 2017. 'The evidential category of mutual knowledge in Quechua'. *Lingua* 186–7: 88–107.

Hintz, Diane M. 2007. 'Past tense forms and their functions in South Conchucos Quechua: time, evidentiality, discourse structure, and affect'. PhD Dissertation, University of California, Santa Barbara.

Holz, Christoph. Forthcoming. 'A comprehensive grammar of Tiang'. PhD thesis, James Cook University.

Hyslop, Gwendolyn. 2014a. 'The grammar of knowledge in Kurtöp: evidentiality, mirativity, and expectation of knowledge', pp. 108–31 of Aikhenvald and Dixon (eds.).
Hyslop, Gwendolyn. 2014b. 'On the category of speaker expectation of interlocutor knowledge in Kurtöp'. Proceedings from the 40th Annual meeting of the Berkeley Linguistics Society, 201–214.
Hyslop, Gwendolyn. 2016. *A grammar of Kurtöp*. Leiden: Brill.
Hyslop, Gwendolyn. 2018a. 'Mirativity and egophoricity in Kurtöp', pp. 109–138 of *Egophoricity*, edited by Simeon Floyd, Elizabeth Norcliffe and Lila San Roque. Amsterdam: John Benjamins.
Hyslop, Gwendolyn. 2018b. 'Evidentiality in Bodic languages', pp. 595–609 of Aikhenvald (ed.).
Hyslop, Gwendolyn. 2020. 'Grammaticalized sources of Kurtöp verbal morphology'. *Studies in Language* 44: 132–64.
Ilyina, L. A. 2017. 'On probable socio-cultural determinants of nonvisual sensory perception evidential grammemes in diachrony of Northern Asian languages'. *Sibirskij filologicheskij zhurnal* 2: 159–74.
Jacobsen, W. H. Jr. 1964. 'A Grammar of the Washo Language'. PhD dissertation, University of California, Berkeley.
Jacobsen, W. H. Jr. 1986. 'The heterogeneity of evidentials in Makah', pp. 3–28 of Chafe and Nichols (eds.).
Jacques, Guillaume. 2018. 'Non-propositional evidentiality', pp. 109–23 of Aikhenvald (ed.).
Jakobson, Roman. 1971. 'Shifters, verbal categories and the Russian verb', pp. 130–43 of his *Selected writings*, vol. 2, *Word and language*, The Hague: Mouton. [Reprinted in Jakobson 1984, 41–58.]
James, D., S. Clarke and M. MacKenzie. 2001. 'The encoding of information source in Algonquian: evidentials in Cree/Montagnais/Naskapi.' *International Journal of American Linguistics* 67: 229–63.
Johanson, Lars. 2003. 'Evidentiality in Turkic', pp. 273–91 of Aikhenvald and Dixon (eds.).
Johanson, Lars. 2018. 'Turkic indirectivity', pp. 510–524 of Aikhenvald (ed.).
Johanson, Lars and Eva Á. Csató. ms. 'On Turkish mnemonic past: an evidential category'.
Johanson, Lars and Bo Utas. 2000. Editors of *Evidentials (Turkic, Iranian and Neighbouring Languages)*. Berlin, New York: Mouton de Gruyter.
Junker, Marie-Odile, Conor M. Quinn, and J. Randolph Valentine. 2018. 'Evidentiality in Algonquian', pp. 431–62 of Aikhenvald (ed.).

Kibrik, A. E. 1977. *Opyt strukturnogo opisanija archinskogo jazuka.* Tom II. *Taksonomicheskaja grammatika.* (An essay in structural description of Archi. Volume II. Taksonomic Grammar). Moscow: Izdateljstvo Moskovskogo Universiteta.

Kibrik, A. E. 1994. 'Archi', pp. 297–365 of *The Indigenous languages of the Caucasus*, Part 2, edited by Rieks Smeets, New York: Caravan Books.

König, Christa. 2013. 'Source of information and unexpected information in !Xun – evidential, mirative and counterexpectation marker', pp. 69–94 of *Linguistic expression of perception and cognition*, edited by Alexandra Aikhenvald and Anne Storch. Leiden: Brill.

Kroeker, Menno. 2001. 'A descriptive grammar of Nambikwara.' *International Journal of American Linguistics* 76: 1–87.

Kroskrity, Paul V. 1993. *Language, history, and identity. Ethnolinguistic studies of the Arizona Tewa.* Tucson and London: The University of Arizona Press.

Kuteva, Tania, Bernd Heine, Bo Hong, Haiping Long, Heiko Narrog, and Seongha Rhee. 2019. *World lexicon of grammaticalization.* Second, extensively revised and updated edition. Cambridge: Cambridge University Press.

Lapenda, G. 1968. *Estrutura da língua Iatê.* Recife: Imprensa Universitária da universidade Federal do Pernambuco.

Laughren, Mary. 1982. 'A preliminary description of propositional particles in Warlpiri', pp. 129–63 of *Papers in Warlpiri grammar: in memory of Lothar Jagst. Work papers of SIL-AAB.* series A, Volume 6, edited by S. Swartz. Darwin: Summer Institute of Linguistics.

Lecarme, Jacqueline. 2008. 'Tense and modality in nominals', pp. 195–225 of *Time and modality*, edited by Jacqueline Guéron and Jacqueline Lecarme. Dordrecht: Springer.

Lee, Dorothy D. 1938. 'Conceptual implications of an Indian language.' *Philosophy of Science* 5: 89–102.

Lee, D. D. 1944. 'Linguistic reflection of Wintu thought.' *International Journal of American Linguistics* 10: 181–7.

Leinonen, Marja. 2000. 'Evidentiality in Komi Zyrian', pp. 419–440 of Johanson and Utas (eds.).

Lidz, Liberty. 2007. 'Evidentiality in Yongning Na (Mosuo)'. *Linguistics of the Tibeto-Burman Area* 30: 45–88.

Lidz, Liberty. 2010. 'A descriptive grammar of Yongning Na (Mosuo)'. PhD dissertation, University of Texas, Austin.

Loeweke, Eunice and Jean May. 1980. 'General grammar of Fasu (Namo Me)', pp. 5–106 of *Grammatical studies in Fasu and Mt. Koiali*, edited by Don Hutchisson. Ukarumpa: Summer Institute of Linguistics, 5–106.

Lowe, Ivan. 1999. 'Nambikwara', pp. 269–92 of *The Amazonian languages,* edited by R. M. W. Dixon and Alexandra Y. Aikhenvald. Cambridge: Cambridge University Press.

Maisak, Timur and Solmaz Merdanova. 2002. 'Kategorija evidencial'nosti v agul'skom jazyke'. *Kavkazovedenie* 1: 102–112.

Malone, Terrell. 1988. 'The Origin and Development of Tuyuca Evidentials'. *International Journal of American Linguistics* 54. 119–40.

Maslova, Elena. 2003. 'Evidentiality in Yukaghir', pp. 219–36 of Aikhenvald and Dixon (eds.).

Matthewson, Lisa. 2004. 'On the methodology of semantic fieldwork'. *International Journal of American Linguistics* 70: 369–415.

Matthewson, Lisa, Henry Davis, and Hotze Rullmann. 2007. 'Evidentials as epistemic modals: Evidence from St'át'imcets'. *Linguistic Variation Yearbook* 7: 201–254.

McLendon, Sally. 2003. 'Evidentials in Eastern Pomo with a comparative survey of the category in other Pomoan languages', pp. 101–30 of Aikhenvald and Dixon (eds.).

Mélac, Eric. 2014. 'L'évidentialité en anglais. Approche contrastive à partir d'un corpus anglais – tibétain'. PhD thesis, Universite Sorbonne Nouvelle – Paris 3.

Mélac, Eric. 2019. 'The grammaticalization of evidentiality in Tibetan'. Ms.

Metslang, H. and K. Pajusalu. 2002. 'Evidentiality in South Estonian.' *Linguistica Uralica* 2: 98–109.

Mihas, Elena I. 2013. 'Non-propositional and verbal temporal morphology in Ashéninka Perené (Arawak)'. *Acta Linguistica Hafniensia* 45: 43–72.

Mihas, Elena I. 2015. *A grammar of Alto Perené (Arawak)*. Berlin: De Gruyter Mouton.

Miller, Cynthia L. and Gilley, Leona G. 2007. 'Evidentiality and mirativity in Shilluk', pp. 191–206 of *Proceedings of the 8th International Nilo-Saharan Linguistics Colloquium*, edited by Mechthild Reh and Doris L. Payne. Cologne: Rüdiger Köppe.

Miller, Marion. 1999. *Desano grammar*. Arlington: Summer Institute of Linguistics and the University of Texas at Arlington.

Mithun, Marianne. 1999. *The Languages of Native North America*. Cambridge: Cambridge University Press.

Molochieva, Zarina and Johanna Nichols. 2018. 'Tense, aspect, mood and evidentiality in Chechen and Ingush', pp. 26–48 of *The semantics of verbal categories in Nakh-Daghestanian languages. Tense, aspect, evidentiality, mood and modality*, edited by Diana Forker and Timur Maisak. Leiden: Brill.

Monserrat, Ruth. 2010. *A língua do povo Mỹky*. Campinas: Editora Curt Nimuendajú.

Monserrat, Ruth and R. M. W. Dixon. 2003. 'Evidentiality in Mỹky', pp. 237–42 of Aikhenvald and Dixon (eds.).

Narrog, Heiko and Wenjiang Yang. 2018. 'Evidentiality in Japanese', pp. 709–724 of Aikhenvald (ed.).

Neukom, L. 2001. *Santali*. Munich: Lincom Europa.

Nichols, Johanna. 2011. *Ingush grammar*. Berkeley: University of California Publications in Linguistics.

Nikolaeva, Irina. 2015. 'On the expression of TAM on nouns: Evidence from Tundra Nenets'. *Lingua* 166: 99–126.

Nordlinger, Rachel and Louisa Sadler. 2004. 'Nominal Tense in Crosslinguistic Perspective'. *Language* 80: 776–806.

Nuckolls, Janis B. 1993. 'The semantics of certainty in Quechua and its implications for a cultural epistemology.' *Language in Society* 22: 235–265.

Nuckolls, Janis B. 2010. *Lessons from a Quechua Strongwoman: Ideophony, Dialogue, and Perspective*. Tucson: University of Arizona Press.

Nuckolls, Janis B. 2018. 'The interactional and cultural pragmatics of evidentiality in Pastaza Quichua', pp. 202–21 of Aikhenvald (ed.).

Nuckolls, Janis B. and Tod D. Swanson. 2014. 'Earthy concreteness and anti-hypotheticalism in Amazonian Quichua discourse'. *Tipiti: Journal of the Society for the Anthropology of Lowland South America*, Volume 12:1. Special Issue edited by Norman E. Whitten Jr. and Michael Uzendoski, available at: http://digitalcommons.trinity.edu/tipiti/vol12/iss1/4.

Nuyts, I. and J. van der Auwera. (eds.). 2015. *The Oxford Handbook of mood and modality*. Oxford: Oxford University Press.

Olawsky, Knut J. 2006. *A grammar of Urarina*. Berlin: Mouton de Gruyter.

Olbertz, Hella. 2007. '*Dizque* in Mexican Spanish: the subjectification of reportative meaning'. *Italian Journal of Linguistics* 19–1: 151–172 (special issue *Evidentiality between lexicon and grammar*, ed. by Mario Squartini).

Oswalt, Robert L. 1986. 'The evidential system of Kashaya', pp. 29–45 of Chafe and Nichols (eds.).

Overall, Simon E. 2014. 'Nominalization, knowledge, and information source in Aguaruna (Jivaroan)', pp. 227–44 of Aikhenvald and Dixon (eds.).

Overall, Simon E. 2017. *A grammar of Aguaruna (Iiniá Chicham)*. Berlin: De Gruyter Mouton.

Palmer, Frank R. 1986. *Mood and Modality*. Cambridge: Cambridge University Press.

Pan, Chia-jung. 2014. 'The grammar of knowledge in Saaroa', pp. 89–106 of Aikhenvald and Dixon (eds.).

Pan, Chia-jung. 2015. 'Reported Evidentials in Saaroa, Kanakanavu, and Tsou', pp. 341–62 of Elizabeth Zeitoun, Stacey F. Teng, and Joy J. Wu (eds.), *New Advances in Formosan Linguistics*. Asia-Pacific Linguistics series studies on Austronesian Languages (SAL 003). The Australian National University, Canberra.

Pan, Chia-jung. 2018. 'Evidentiality in Formosan languages', pp. 657–673 of Aikhenvald (ed.).

Payne, Thomas E. and Doris L. Payne. 2007. *A typological grammar of Panare, a Cariban language of Venezuela*. Leiden: Brill.

Perrot, J. R. 1996. 'Un médiatif ouralien: l'auditif en Samoyède Nenets', pp. 157–68 of *L'Énonciation médiatisée*, edited by Zlatka Guentchéva. Louvain – Paris: Éditions Peeters.

Peterson, Tyler. 2018. 'Evidentiality and epistemic modality in Gitksan', pp. 463–489 of Aikhenvald (ed.).

Pitkin, Harvey. 1984. *Wintu grammar*. Berkeley: University of California Press.
Ramirez, Henri. 1997. *A Fala Tukano dos Yepâ-masa. Tomo I. Gramática*. Manaus: Inspetoria Salesiana Missionária da Amazônia CEDEM.
Ramirez, Henri. 2001. *Uma gramática do Baniwa do Içana*. Manaus: UFAm.
de Reuse, W. J. 2003. 'Evidentiality in Western Apache', pp. 79–100 of Aikhenvald and Dixon (eds.).
Routamaa, Judy. 1994. *Kamula grammar essentials*. Ms. Ukarumpa: Summer Institute of Linguistics.
Rule, William Murray. 1977. 'A comparative study of the Foe, Huli and Pole languages of Papua New Guinea'. PhD thesis, University of Sydney.
Sarvasy, Hannah. 2018. 'Evidentiality in the languages of New Guinea', pp. 629–656 of Aikhenvald (ed.).
Scatton, Ernest A. 1984. *A reference grammar of Modern Bulgarian*. Columbus, OH: Slavica.
Schlichter, Alice. 1986. 'The Origin and Deictic Nature of Wintu Evidentials', pp. 46–59 of Chafe and Nichols (eds.).
Seki, L. 2000. *Gramática do Kamaiurá, língua Tupí-Guaraní do Alto Xingu*. Campinas: Editora da Unicamp.
Shipley, W. F. 1964. *Maidu grammar*. Berkeley and Los Angeles: University of California Press.
Shirai, S. 2007. 'Evidential and evidential-like categories in nDrapa'. *Linguistics of the Tibeto-Burman Area* 30(2): 125–50.
Sillitoe, P. 2010. 'Trust in development: some implications of knowing in indigenous knowledge.' *The Journal of the Royal Anthropological Institute* 16: 12–30.
Skribnik. Elena and Petar Kehayov. 2018. 'Evidentiality in Uralic languages', pp. 525–553 of Aikhenvald (ed.).
Skribnik. Elena and Olga Seesing. 2014. 'Evidentiality in Kalmyk', pp. 148–70 of Aikhenvald and Dixon (eds.).
Slobin, Dan I. 1996. 'From "thought and language" to "thinking for speaking"', pp. 70–96 of *Rethinking linguistic relativity*, edited by John J. Gumperz and Stephen C. Levinson. Cambridge: Cambridge University Press.
Slobin, Dan I. and A. A. Aksu-Koç. 1982. 'Tense, Aspect, and Modality in the use of the Turkish evidential', pp. 185–200 of *Tense-Aspect: Between Semantics and Pragmatics*, edited by P. J. Hopper. Amsterdam: John Benjamins.
Smeets, I. 2007. *Mapuche*. Berlin: Mouton de Gruyter.
Sohn, Ho-min. 2018. 'Evidentiality in Korean', pp. 693–709 of Aikhenvald (ed.).
Soto Ruiz, Clodoaldo. 1979. *Quechua. Manual de Enseñanza*. Instituto de Estudios Peruanos. Lima.
Stenzel, Kristine and Elsa Gomez-Imbert. 2018. 'Evidentiality in Tukanoan languages', pp. 357–87 of Aikhenvald (ed.).

Storch, Anne. 1999. *Das Hone und seine Stellung in Zentral-Jukunoid*. Köln: Rudiger Köppe Verlag.

Storch, Anne. 2009. 'Hone (Jukun)', pp. 123–40 of *Coding Participant Marking. Construction Types in Twelve African Languages*, edited by Gerrit I. Dimmendaal. Amsterdam: Benjamins.

Storch, Anne. 2018. 'Evidentiality and the expression of knowledge: An African perspective', pp. 610–28 of Aikhenvald (ed.).

Storch, Anne. Forthcoming. Tense and aspect in Wapha (Jukun, Nigeria).

Storch, Anne and Coly, Jules Jacques. 2014. 'The grammar of knowledge in Maaka (Western Chadic, Nigeria)', pp. 190–208 of Aikhenvald and Dixon (eds.).

Sun, Jackson T.-S. 1993. 'Evidentials in Amdo Tibetan'. *Bulletin of the Institute of History and Philology, Academia Sinica* 63 (4): 945–1001.

Sun, Jackson T.-S. 2018. 'Evidentials and person', pp. 47–64 of Aikhenvald (ed.).

Tatevosov, S. G. 2001. 'From resultatives to evidentials: multiple uses of the perfect in Nakh-Daghestanian languages'. *Journal of Pragmatics* 33: 443–64.

Telban, Borut. 2014. 'Saying, seeing and knowing among the Karawari of Papua New Guinea', pp. 260–77 of Aikhenvald and Dixon (eds.).

Telles, Stella and W. Leo Wetzels. 2006. 'Evidentiality and Epistemic Mood in Lakondê', pp. 235–52 of *What's in a Verb? Studies in the Verbal Morphology of the Languages of the Americas*, edited by Grażyna J. Rowicka and Eithne B. Carlin. Utrecht, The Netherlands: LOT Publications.

Thiesen, Wesley and David J. Weber. 2012. *A grammar of Bora, with special attention to tone*. Dallas, Texas: SIL International.

Thurgood, Graham. 1986. 'The Nature and Origins of the Akha Evidentials System', pp. 214–22 of Chafe and Nichols (eds.).

Tipton, Ruth A. 1982. *Nembi procedural and narrative discourse*. Canberra: Pacific Linguistics.

Tournadre, Nicolas. 2004. 'Typologie des aspects verbaux et intégration à une théorie du TAM'. *Bulletin de la Société Linguistique de Paris* XCIX, fasc. 1: 7–68.

Tournadre, Nicolas. 2011. 'Le tibétain', pp. 1040–9 of *Dictionnaire des langues*, edited by E. Bonvini, J. Busuttil & A. Peyraube. Paris: Presses Universitaires de France.

Tournadre, N. and K. Jiatso, K. 2001. 'Final auxiliary verbs in literary Tibetan and in the dialects'. *Linguistics of the Tibeto-Burman Area* 24: 49–111.

Travis, Catherine. 2006. Dizque: a Colombian evidentiality strategy. *Linguistics* 44: 1269–97.

Valenzuela, Pilar M. 2003. 'Evidentiality in Shipibo-Konibo, with a Comparative Overview of the Category in Panoan', pp. 33–61 of Aikhenvald and Dixon (eds.).

Vallauri, E. L. 2004. 'Grammaticalization of syntactic incompleteness: free conditionals in Italian and other languages'. *SKY Journal of Linguistics* 17: 189–215.

van der Voort, Hein. 2004. *A grammar of Kwaza*. Berlin: Mouton de Gruyter.

Vanrell, Maria del Mar, Meghan Armstrong, and Pilar Prieto. 2014. 'The role of prosody in the encoding of evidentiality'. Presentation at the 7th International Conference on Speech Prosody.

Wälchli, Bernard. 2000. 'Infinite predication as marker of evidentiality and modality in the languages of the Baltic region'. *Sprachtypologie und Universalienforschung* 53: 186–210.

Wangdi, Pema. Forthcoming. 'A grammar of Brokpa'. PhD thesis, James Cook University.

Watters, Stephen. 2018. 'A grammar of Dzongkha (dzo): phonology, words, and simple clauses'. PhD dissertation, Rice University, Houston, Texas.

Watters, Stephen. ms. 'The cultural, ecological and sociolinguistic context'.

Weber, David J. 1989. *A grammar of Huallaga (Huánuco) Quechua*. Berkeley: University of California Press.

Whistler, Kenneth W. 1986. 'Evidentials in Patwin', pp. 60–74 of Chafe and Nichols (eds.).

Widmer, Manuel. 2017. 'The evolution of egophoricity and evidentiality in the Himalayas: the case of Bunan'. *The rise and development of evidential and epistemic markers*. Special issue of *Journal of Historical Linguistics* 7: 246–275.

Wiemer, Björn. 2006. 'Grammatical evidentiality in Lithuanian (a typological assessment)'. *Baltistica* 41.1: 33–49.

Wiemer, Björn. 2018. 'Evidentials and epistemic modality', pp. 85–108 of Aikhenvald (ed.).

Wilcox, Shgerman and Barbara Shaffer. 2018. 'Evidentiality and information source in signed languages', pp. 741–54 of Aikhenvald (ed.).

Wilkins, D. P. 1989. 'Mparntwe Arrernte (Aranda): Studies in the Structure and Semantics of Grammar'. PhD dissertation, ANU, Canberra.

Willett, Thomas. 1988. 'A cross-linguistic survey of the grammaticalization of evidentiality'. *Studies in Language* 12: 51–97.

Willis, Christina M. 2007. 'Evidentiality in Darma (Tibeto-Burman)'. *Linguistics of the Tibeto-Burman Area* 30: 45–88.

Willis, Christina Oko. 2019. *A grammar of Darma*. Leiden: Brill.

Wiltschko, Martina. 2003. 'On the interpretability of tense on D and its consequences for case theory'. *Lingua* 113: 659–696.

Wojtylak, Katarzyna I. 2018. 'Evidentiality in Boran and Witotoan languages', pp. 388–408 of Aikhenvald (ed.).

Wood, Michael. 2018. 'Stereotypes and evidentiality', pp. 243–57 of Aikhenvald (ed.).

Yang, Gloria Fan-pei. 2000a. 'The semantics-pragmatics of the hearsay evidential *nana* in Tsou', *National Taiwan University Working Papers in Linguistics* 3: 69–86.

Yang, Gloria Fan-pei. 2000b. 'Tsou case markers as evidentials', *National Taiwan University Working Papers in Linguistics* 3: 41–67.

Yap, Foong-Ha, K. Grunow-Hårsta and J. Wrona. 2011. *Nominalization in Asian languages: Diachronic and typological perspectives*. Amsterdam: John Benjamins.
Zeisler, Bettina. 2011. *Relative tense and aspectual values in Tibetan languages. A comparative study*. Berlin: De Gruyter Mouton.
Zhang, Sihong. 2014. 'The expression of knowledge in Ersu', pp. 132–47 of Aikhenvald and Dixon (eds.).
Zhang, Sihong. 2016. *A grammar of Ersu*. Munich: Lincom Europa.
Ziegeler, Deborah. 2011. 'The grammaticalization of modality', pp. 595–604 of *The Oxford Handbook of Grammaticalization*, edited by Heiko Narrog and Bernd Heine. Oxford: Oxford University Press.
Zúñiga, Fernando. ms. Some notes on the Mapudungun evidential.

Books by Alexandra Y. Aikhenvald

Strukturno-tipologichskaja klassifikacija berberskih jazykov. (A structural and typological classification of Berber languages) 3 issues (in Russian).
Sovremennyj Ivrit. (Modern Hebrew.) (in Russian).
Bare.
Tariana Texts and Cultural Context.
Manual da língua tariana. Histórias tariana.
Classifiers. A Typology of Noun Categorization Devices.
Dicionário Tariana-Português e Português-Tariana.
Language Contact in Amazonia.
A grammar of Tariana, from northwest Amazonia.
Evidentiality.
The Manambu language, from East Sepik, Papua New Guinea.
Imperatives and commands.
The languages of the Amazon.
The art of grammar: a practical guide.
How gender shapes the world.
Serial verbs.
I saw the dog: How language works.

with R. M. W. Dixon
Language at large. Essays in syntax and semantics.

Edited books and special issues of journals
Nominal classification, Special issue of Sprachtypologie und Universalienforschung 57 2/3. 329 pp.
Linguistic fieldwork, Special issue of Sprachtypologie und Universalienforschung, volume 60, 1.
Evidentiality, a special issue of Linguistics of Tibeto-Burman Area 30.2.
The Oxford Handbook of evidentiality.

with R. M. W. Dixon
The Amazonian Languages.
Changing Valency: Case Studies in Transitivity.
Areal diffusion and genetic inheritance: problems in comparative linguistics.
Word: a cross-linguistic typology.
Studies in evidentiality.
Adjectives: a cross-linguistic typology.
Serial verb constructions: a crosslinguistic typology.
Complementation: a cross-linguistic typology.
Grammars in contact: a cross-linguistic typology.
Semantics of clause linking: a crosslinguistic typology.
Possession and ownership: a cross-linguistic typology.
The grammar of knowledge: a cross-linguistic typology.
The Cambridge Handbook of Linguistic Typology.
Commands: a cross-linguistic typology.

with R. M. W. Dixon and Nerida Jarkey
The integration of language and society: a cross-linguistic typology

with R. M. W. Dixon and Masayuki Onishi
Non-canonically marked subjects and objects.

with R. M. W. Dixon and Nathan M. White
Phonological and grammatical word: a cross-linguistic typology.

with Péter Maitz
Contact languages and blended grammars. Special issue of Italian Journal of Linguistics.

with Elena Mihas
Genders and classifiers: a cross-linguistic typology.

with Pieter Muysken
Multiverb constructions: a view from the Americas.

with Anne Storch
Perception and cognition in language and culture.
Taboo in language and discourse. Special issue of Mouth 4.

with Anne Storch, Andrea Hollington, and Nico Nassenstein
Creativity in language: secret codes and special styles. A special issue of the International Journal of Language and Culture 6.1.

Index

Abkhaz   19, 82, 89, 100, 109
access to information, *see* addressee, information source of, egophoricity
addressee dative pronouns   40–1
addressee, information source of   8, 16–17, 40–1, 66–73, 78–81, 87, 91–5, 106–12, *see also* egophoricity
Adelaar, Willem F. H.   16–17, 24, 72–4, 89
admirative   16
Aguaruna   37, 101–2
Agul   86
Akha   36, 55–6, 82, 100
Aksu-Koç, A. A.   28
Albanian   16, 100
Alcázar, Asier   6, 46–7, 61, 101–2
Algonquian languages   25, 82, 92, 99
alterphoric   36–7
Alto Perené   53
Amazonian languages   51, 61, 100
Amazonian Portuguese   31, 61, 83–4
Amazonian Spanish   61, 84
anterior   100–1
apprehensive   109
Arakaki, Tomoko   98
Arawá languages   9, 42, *see also* Jarawara
Arawak languages   8, 10, 22, 53, *see also* Alto Perené, Baniwa of Içana, Tariana
Archi   30, 85, 100
areal diffusion   8, 62, 80, 87
Arizona Tewa   7
Armstrong, Meghan   3

Ashéninka Perené   103
aspect   1–2, 13, 18, 21, 84–5, 93, 88–9, *see also* imperfective aspect, perfect, perfective aspect, past tense, present tense
assertion   19
assumed evidential   10, 31, 59, 76–83, 86–8, 92, 111, *see also* assumption
assumption   2, 4, 7, 10–12, 14, 32, 37–8, 70, 76–80, 87, 101, 106, *see also* inference
attitude to knowledge   1, 2, 7, 18–21, 59, *see also* epistemic modality
auditive   60, 105
auditory information   14, 41, 68, 89, 98
Australian languages   96–7, 104, *see also* Dyirbal, Mparntwe Arrernte, Warlbiri
Ayacucho Quechua   73
Aymara   7, *see also* Jaqi

Bai, Junwei   15–17, 20, 36, 68
Balkans as a linguistic area   8, 100
Baniwa of Içana   8–10, 44–5, 87, 91, 94–5, 103
Baraby, Anne-Marie   92
Barasano   89, 93
Barbacoan languages   31, 36, 52
Barnes, Janet   11, 86
Bashkir   7, 27
Benue-Congo languages   40
Bergqvist, Henrik   68
Bertinetto, Pier Marco   5, 48, 103
Bo Hong   21, 82
Boas, Frans   3–5

Bodic languages   20, see also Bodish languages
Bodish languages   20, 44, 6
Boi'nun   95
Bora   57, 81, 92
Bora-Witotoan languages   92
borrowing   5, see also areal diffusion, language contact
Bosavi languages   54
Brokpa   42, 96
Brosig, Benjamin   37, 54, 64–5, 93
Brown, P.   114
Bulgarian   44, 89–90
Bullock, A.   20
Bunte, P. A.   83
Buryat   37–8, 65, 110

Campbell, Lyle   102
Carib languages   60, 98, 102
Carlin, Eithne B.   60, 98, 109
Carol, Javier J.   45, 104
case   2, 20, 48, 84, 102, 105–9
Cavineña   89, 95
Central Pomo   68
certainty   18–19, 23–4, 36–8, 51, 64, 82, 100, see also epistemic modality, uncertainty
Chadic languages   38, 48, 106
Chafe, Wallace L.   5
Chang, Henry   48
change in evidential use   61
Chechen   40–1
Chepang   36
Chirikba, V.   89. 100, 109
Chorote   45, 104
Chung, Sandra   20
Circassian   82, 100
Clarke, S.   25, 82, 100
Colombian Spanish   6, 30–1, 46–7
Coly, Jules Jacques   38, 45, 48, 69, 106
command   5, 85, 90–7, 109, see also directive, imperative
common knowledge evidential   63–5, 68, 78, 81, see also general knowledge
complement clause   6, 43–4, 89, 102
complementizer   6
Comrie, Bernard   88
Conchucos Quechua   71–2, 110

conditional   6, 37, 43, 89–90, 99, 106, 126
conjecture   3, 12, 72, see also inferred evidential
conjunct/disjunct person marking   16, 36 see also egophoricity
contact language, see also Amazonian Portuguese, Amazonian Spanish, areal diffusion, language contact
control   15, 23, 30–4, 109
converb   7, 100
copula   33–5, 100–2
counter-expectation   16–17, 38, 53
Cree/Montagnais/Naskapi   25, 82, 99–100
Csató, Eva Á.   54
cultural conventions in evidential use   61–2, see also metalinguistic awareness of evidentials
Cupeño   35
Curnow, Timothy Jowan   22
Cuzco Quechua   74

Daguman, Josephine   43, 93, 95
Dardic languages   30
Darma   81
Davis, Henry   83
De Haan, Ferdinand   5
de Reuse, W. J.   33–4
de-subordination   101–2
declarative   76, 85, 90–92, 95, see also assertion, indicative, speech act
deduction   31, 82, see also assumption, inference
deductive approach   12
deferred realisation   33–4, 109
definiteness   3, 100, 107–8, see also topicality
deictic   104, see also demonstrative
DeLancey, Scott   14, 16–17, 20, 35, 88, 112
demonstrative   41, 104–5, 109
Dendale, Patrick   6, 37
deontic modality   37, 89
dependent clause   40–3, 55, 89–90, 101–2
diachronic development of evidentials, see historical development of evidentials
Dickinson, Connie   31, 36. 52
direct evidential   23–4, 27, 35–6, 49, 52, 60, 69, 72–4, 92, see also eyewitness evidential, firsthand evidential
direct speech   26, see also speech report

directive 97, *see also* command, imperative, speech act
discourse 12, 40, 60–2, 109–12, *see also* genre
disjunct person marking, *see* conjunct/disjunct person marking
distal visual evidential 13, 48, 105
Dixon, R. M. W. 3, 5, 9–10, 16, 22, 28, 42–8, 57, 60–1, 84–5, 90, 97
dizque as a marker of information source in Spanish and Portuguese 6, 30–1, 46–8, 61, 83–4
Doble, Marion 73
double marking of information source 39, 49–52, 81, 110
doubt, *see* dubitative, epistemic modality
Dozon, A. 16
dreams, evidentials in 8, 12, 57, 75
dubitative 18, 48, 53, 82–4, 89, 99–100, *see also* epistemic modality
Dyirbal 45, 60, 104

East Tukanoan languages 11, 13, 19, 32, 53, 61, 80, 84–9
Eastern Pomo 44, 51, 93
Eberhard, David M. 13, 23–4, 27, 32, 48, 61, 65–71, 80, 88, 92, 99, 104, 108–11
Egerod, S. 55
egophoric, *see* egophoricity
egophoricity 2, 14–16, 19–23, 35–45, 52–5, 59, 62–80, 110–12
Ekari 73
empathy 26, 112
endangered language 71, 72, *see also* language obsolescence
endopathic expressions 23
endophoric expressions 63, *see also* egophoricity
Engan languages 73
English 7–8, 19, 44, 53, 82–3, 97, 111
epistemic extensions of evidentials 20, 23–8, 48, 81, *see also* epistemic modality, evidentiality strategy
epistemic modality 2, 7–8, 18–28, 36–8, 40–2, 45, 48, 51–3, 59–64, 68–70, 81–4, 88–9, 96, 99–100, 109–10, *see also* certainty, uncertainty
epistemology 20
Ersu 49–50, 88, 110

Estonian 18, 22, 27, 43–4, 89–90, 98, *see also* South Estonian, Standard Estonian
European languages 8, 18–20, *see also* Indo-European languages
Evenki 21
evidence, as inappropriate in defining evidentiality 5–6
evidential marking on nouns 13, 41, 45–9, 55, 68–9, 85, 103–9, *see also* non-propositional evidentiality
evidentiality strategy 6, 20–2, 37, 81, 87, 101
evidentiality, definition of 2–14
evidentially-neutral form 24, 43, 109
evidentials in dreams *see* dreams, evidentials in
exclamation 90
expectation of knowledge, *see* mirativity
experiential evidential 24, 55, 82, 105, *see also* direct evidential, sensory evidential
eyewitness evidential 11, 28, 45–6, *see also* direct evidential, firsthand evidential

Faller, Martina 45, 74
Fasu 73
Finno-Ugric languages 93, 100
first person effect 22, *see also* egophoricity
firsthand evidential 9, 13–14, 24–5, 46, 60, 72, 90–1, 104, *see also* direct evidential, non-firsthand evidential
firsthand information, *see* firsthand evidential
Fleck, David 42, 55, 88–9
Floyd, Rick 23, 33, 56
Floyd, Simeon 8
focus 38, 109
Foe 54, 73, 88
Forest Enets 101
Forker, Diana 23, 30, 86. 89, 100
Formosan languages 30, 46–7, 105
Frajzyngier, Zygmunt 24
French 6, 37, 99
Friedman, Victor 6–8, 16, 20, 44, 81, 89, 99–100
frustrative modality 18
Furbee, N. Louanna 7
future 3, 52–4, 81–2, 86, 89, 99–100

Galloway, Brent D. 103
García Salido, Gabriela 69

Gawne, L.   20, 35
general knowledge   10, 27, 32, 63–71, 74, 78–81, 87–8, 108–10
genre   39, 59–62, 97, 110–11, *see also* discourse
Georgian   88
Gerzenstein, Anna   104
Gilley, Leona G.   90
Gipper, Sonja   81
Goddard, C.   97
Gomez-Imbert, Elsa   13, 19, 32, 54, 80, 84-, 86, 89, 93
grammatical evidentiality, essence of   4–13
grammaticalization of evidentiality   2–7, 10–12, 18–20, 30, 50–1, 64–5, 68, 81–2, 85, 10
Greed, Teija   7, 21, 24, 27, 29, 86, 90, 100
Gronemeyer, C.   101
Grosh, Andrew   54
Grosh, Sylvia   54
Grunow-Hårsta, K.   101
Gruzdeva, E. Ju.   91
Grzech, Karolina   24
Guillaume, Antoine   89, 113
Gutiérrez, Analía   45, 104

habitual   64–7
Haiping Long   21, 82
Halkomelem   103
Hansson, I-L.   55
Hardman, M. J.   7
Hargreaves, David   16
Harris, Alice C.   102
Haspelmath, Martin   86
hearsay   17, 31, 44, 73, 80–2, 100–1, *see also* reported evidential, quotative evidential, secondhand evidential, thirdhand evidential
   in non-propositional evidentiality   107
Hein, Veronika   35
Heine, Bernd   4, 21, 82
Hill Patwin   82, 100
Hill, Jane H.   35, 62
Hill, Nathan W.   20, 35
Hintz, Daniel J.   71–2
Hintz, Diane M.   71–2
Hinuq   23, 30, 60, 85, 89

historical development of evidentials   3, 6, 81–5, 99–103, 109, *see also* grammaticalization of evidentiality, language contact, reanalysis, reinterpretation
Holz, Christoph   41
Hone   40–1, 45, 62
Huallaga Quechua   24
Hyslop, Gwendolyn   16–17, 19–20, 36, 81, 88

Iatê   48
Ilonggo   46, 48, 95, 103
Ilyina, L. A.   60
imperative   5, 90–2, 96–7, *see also* command, directive
imperfective aspect   88–89, *see also* aspect
implicature   24
indicative   24, 89, *see also* declarative
indirect evidential   23, 27, 37, 81, 100, *see also* non-eyewitness evidential, non-firsthand evidential
indirect speech   7
Indo-European languages   83
inference   2, 4–7, 11–14, 24, 31–4, 49–51, 54–5, 87–9, 100–1, *see also* inferential evidential, inferred evidential
inferential evidential   31–5, 63, 68–72, 81–2, 89, 107–8, *see also* inferred evidential
inferred evidential   10, 19, 27, 32, 49–55, 65, 77, 83, 87–8, 101, 108, *see also* inferential evidential, inference
information source   6, 9, 30, 33, 81–2, *see also* evidentiality, definition of
Ingush   40–1, 45, 68
Innu   92
interjection   41, 112
internal state   23, 26, 63, 77, 110
interrogative forms   41, 68, 92–5, *see also* questions
intersubjectivity   111–2
intonation   37
irrealis   111–12, *see also* realis, reality status
Irvine, J. T.   62

Jacobsen, W. H. Jr.   5, 31
Jacques, Guillaume   13, 45, 48, 104
Jakobson, Roman   5, 89

James, D. 82, 100
Japanese 56, 123
Jaqi 7
Jarawara 9, 18, 28, 42, 45, 48–9, 57, 84–5, 89–90, 103
Jarkey, Nerida 3, 61
Jiatso, K. 16
Jivaroan languages 37, 101
Johanson, Lars 5, 23, 54, 93, 100, 109
joint perception 70, 106, see also shared knowledge in evidentials
Jukunoid languages 40, 62
Junker, Marie-Odile 82, 92

Kalasha 30
Kalmyk 54, 64–5, 88, 90, 93, 97, 110
Kaluli 54
Kamaiurá 13, 101
Kamula 54
Karawari 7
Kashaya 34, 68, 89, 98
Kayardild 48
Kehayov, Petar 43, 81, 90, 94, 101
Kendall, M. B. 83
Khalkha 93
Khwarshi 30
Kibrik, A. E. 16, 30
Komi 101
König, Christa 4, 89, 109
Korean 54
Kotiria, see Wanano
Kroeker, Menno 67, 70
Kroskrity, Paul V. 7
Kurtöp 19, 36, 81, 88
Kuteva, Tania 21, 44, 82
Kutubuan languages 54
Kwaza 52

Lakondê 13, 48, 71, 88, 104
language contact 8, 62, 80, see areal diffusion, borrowing, Vaupés River Basin linguistic area
language obsolescence 68, 71, 80–4, 111, see also endangered language
Lapenda, G. 48
Latin American Spanish 103, see also Colombian Spanish

Latvian 102
Laughren, Mary 96
Lecarme, Jacqueline 48
Lee, Dorothy D. 59, 82
Lega 109
Leinonen, Marja 101
Levinson, S. C. 114
lexical expression of information source 2–6, 18, 58, 61, 76, 83–4
Lezgi 86, 100
Lezgic 86
Lhasa Tibetan 22, 35–6, 49–50, 52, 88
Lidz, Liberty 50–1, 60, 63–4, 68
Língua Geral, see Nhêengatú
Lithuanian 101
Loeweke, Eunice 73
Lowe, Ivan 45, 70, 107–8

Maaka 38, 45, 48, 69–70, 106–9
Macedonian 7, 44
MacKenzie, M. 25, 82, 100
Macro-Jê languages 48
Maidu 91
Maisak, Timur 86
Maká 104
Malone, Terrell 101
Mamaindê 13, 23–4, 27–8, 32, 61, 65–71, 78, 87, 92, 108, 110
Manambu 41
Mapudungun 28–9
Mari 93–4
markedness 8, 13–14, 24, 77, 81, 104
Maslova, Elena 34
Mataco-Mataguayan languages 45, 104
Matses 51, 55, 85, 88–9
Matthewson, Lisa 12, 83
May, Jean 73
Mayan languages 7
McLendon, Sally 74, 51, 68, 93
Mélac, Eric 35–6, 50–1, 57, 81
Merdanova, Solmaz 86
metalinguistic awareness of evidentials 58–9
Metslang, H. 100
Mihas, Elena I. 53, 103
Miller, Cynthia L. 104
Miller, Marion 80

mirativity   1–2, 16–21, 28–39, 42–5, 52–3, 59–62, 81, 100, 110–12
   in pronouns   40–1
Mithun, Marianne   68
modal verb   3, 7-, 83, 96, 111
modality, see deontic modality, epistemic modality
mode   7, 20
Molochieva, Zarina   40–1
Mongolian   93
Mongolic languages   37
Monguor   93
Monserrat, Ruth   97
mood   21, 85, 90, 100, 108, see also sentence type, speech act
Mparntwe Arrernte   97
Munda languages   104–5
Munya   15, 17, 36, 68
Murui   81
Mỹky   97

Nakh-Daghestanian languages   40, 85–6, 100
Nambiquara languages   13, 24, 27, 45, 48, 61, 65–70, 80, 87–8, 104
Narrog, Heiko   4, 21, 56–7, 82
Nassenstein, Nico   7
nDrapa   35
Ndu languages   41
negation   1–2, 39, 55–7, 62, 84, 94–100, 110
Nembi   73
Nenets   48, 60, 81, 101, see also Tundra Nenets
Neukom, L.   104–5
New Guinea, languages of   20, 41, 54, 73, 88
Newari   36
Nhêengatú   8
Nichols, Johanna   5, 40–1, 68
Nikolaeva, Irina   48
Nivaĉle   54, 104
Nivkh   91
nominal aspect   48, 103
nominal evidentiality, see non-propositional evidentiality
nominal tense   103, 107–8
nominalisation   21, 33, 81, 98, 101–2, see also evidentiality strategy
non-declarative   85, 89, 95–7, see also speech act

non-experiential evidential   105, see also indirect evidential, non-eyewitness evidential, non-firsthand evidential
non-eyewitness evidential   10, 24, 28, 29, see also indirect evidential, non-firsthand evidential
non-finite form   98, 102
non-firsthand evidential   9–10, 14, 24–5, 28–30, 33–4, 37, 46, 82, 86–7, 92–4, 99–103, see also firsthand evidential, indirect evidential
non-indicative mood   100, 103, see also mood, sentence type, speech act
non-propositional evidentiality   13, 41, 45–9, 55, 68–9, 85
non-witnessed forms   6, 27, 44, 60, 74, 98, 109, see also non-eyewitness evidential
nonvisual evidential   10–14, 22–6, 32, 37, 48, 57–61, 65, 68–71, 75–7, 82–3, 86–105, 110, see also direct evidential, non-eyewitness evidential, visual evidential
Nordlinger, Rachel   48
North-East Caucasian languages   16, 30, 89
Northern Kankanay   93
Northern Khanty   30
Northwest Caucasian languages   82, 100
noun phrase, evidentials in, see non-propositional evidentiality
Nuckolls, Janis B.   6–7, 19, 24
Nuyts, I.   18

O'dam, see Southern Tepehuan
Oceanic languages   41
Olawsky, Knut J.   97
Olbertz, Hella   47
omission of evidentials   13
origin of evidentials   4, 6, 13, 50, 55, 82, 100–2, 111, see also grammaticalization of evidentiality, historical development of evidentials, reanalysis, reinterpretation
Oswalt, Robert L.   34, 68, 89
Overall, Simon E.   37, 101

Pajusalu, K.   100
Palmer, Frank R.   18, 20, 83
Pan, Chia-jung   46–7, 90, 93, 95–6, 105

Panare   102
Panoan languages   27, 55, 89, 92
Papuan languages   7, *see also* New Guinea, languages of
parenthetical   3, 7, 112
participle   64–5, 92, 101–2
past tense   9, 18, 26, 30, 42, 45–6, 53–4, 58, 65, 78, 100–1, *see also* present tense
Pastaza Quichua   6–7, 19, 24
Payne, Doris L.   102
Payne, Thomas E.   102
perfect   89, 97, 101–3
perfective aspect   21, 40, 88–9, *see also* imperfective aspect, perfect
Perrot, J. R.   101
person   14–16, 22–3, 28–40, 71–3, 84–5, 98–9, *see also* conjunct/disjunct person marking, first person effect, speech act participant (SAP)
personal knowledge   22, 35, 88, 100, 112, *see also* egophoricity
Peterson, Tyler   83
Philippine languages   46, 93, 95, 103
Piratapuya   32–3
Pitkin, Harvey   82
polarity, *see* negation
politeness   85, 95–7, 109
Pomoan languages   68, 89, 93
Portuguese   6, 18, 31, 61, 77–8, 83, *see also* Amazonian Portuguese
precision, requirement for   4, 6, 61–3, 83, 110, *see also* cultural conventions in evidential use
preferred evidential choice   11–12, 75–8
present tense   18, 54, 65–6, 74–7, 86–9, 101–2, 108, *see also* past tense
Prieto, Pilar   3
prospective evidential   81
Proto-Algonquian   100
proximal visual evidential   13, 48, 105

Quechua, *see* Ayacucho Quechua, Conchucos Quechua, Cuzco Quechua, Huallaga Quechua, Pastaza Quichua, Quechuan languages, Sihuas Quechua, Tarma Quechua, Tena Kichwa, Wanka Quechua
Quechuan languages   6, 16, 24, 33, 44, 72–4

questions   9, 15–16, 36–9, 56–62, 68, 92–7, 100, *see also* interrogative forms
Qiangic languages   35
Quinn, Conor M.   82, 92
quotation   7, 50, 64, *see also* direct speech, reported speech, speech report
quotative evidential   107

Ramirez, Henri   8, 54, 77, 86, 89, 93, 103
realis   11–12, *see also* irrealis, reality status
reality status   21, 48, 93–112, *see also* irrealis, realis
reanalysis   99–102
reasoning   4, 12, 77, 80, *see also* assumed evidential
reinterpretation   81–2, 99, 102, 104, 111, *see also* reanalysis
relative clause   42–4, 48–51, 89–90
reliability   4–7, 18–19, 24, 28, 61, 68–70, 110–11, *see also* epistemic modality
reportative evidential   35, 57, 65, 84, 95, *see also* reported evidential
reported evidential   6–14, 17–19, 24–33, 42–59, 72, 76, 80–90, 106–10, *see also* hearsay, secondhand evidential, thirdhand evidential
reported information   12, 24, 28–33, 43, 54, 60, 69–72, 83, 86, 92, 97
reported speech   30–1, *see also* direct speech, indirect speech, speech report
responsibility   37, 111
resultative   6, 100–3
Romance languages   6
Routamaa, Judy   54
Rule, William Murray   73
Rullmann, Hotze   83
Russian   97
Ryukyuan   98

Saaroa   30, 90, 95
Sabanê   88
Sadler, Louisa   48
Salish languages   103
Samoyedic languages   60, 81, 85, 101
Santali   104–5
Sarvasy, Hannah   53, 73, 88
Scatton, Ernest A.   89

Schlichter, Alice 82
scope of egophoricity 40–1, 62
scope of evidentials 5, 13, 39–51, 55–9, 62–4, 70, *see also* non-propositional evidentiality
scope of mirativity 40–1, 62
scope of negation 55, 57
secondhand evidential 7–9, 12–14, 27, 49–51, 63–5, 86–9, 94–5, 98, 106–8, *see also* reported evidential
Seesing, Olga 54, 64, 88, 90, 97
Seki, L. 13, 101
sensory evidential 12, 14, 82–3, 88, 93, 103, *see also* visual evidential, non-visual evidential
sentence type 90–7, *see also* declarative, imperative, interrogative form, mood, non-declarative, speech act
Seongha Rhee 21, 82
Shaffer, Barbara 3
shamans 12, 57–60, 74–6, *see also* sorcery, spirits, supernatural experience
shared knowledge in evidentials 63, 66–70, 72–81, 88, *see also* assumed evidential, general knowledge
Shilluk 90
Shipibo-Konibo 18, 22, 27–8, 31, 42, 45, 60, 74, 90, 92, 96
Shipley, W. F. 91
Shirai, S. 35
signed languages 3
Sihuas Quechua 72, 110
Sillitoe, P. 73
Sissala 109
Skribnik, Elena 37, 43, 54, 65, 81, 88, 90, 93–4, 97, 101
Slavic languages 89
Slobin, Dan I. 3, 28
Smeets, I. 28
Sohn, Ho-min 54
sorcery 74, 83, *see also* shamans, spirits, supernatural experience
Soto Ruiz, Clodoaldo 73
South Estonian 100
South-Caucasian languages 88
Southern Nambikwara 67, 70–1, 78, 87, 107–10
Southern Tepehuan 69

Spanish 6, 19, 30–1, 46–7, 61, 83–4, 103, *see also* Amazonian Spanish, Colombian Spanish
speculation 27, 37, 85, 96–7, 100
speech act 85, 89, 97, *see also* mood, sentence type
speech act participant (SAP) 15, 72–3, 77, 93, *see also* egophoricity, person
speech report 3, 7–13, 21, 26–8, 46, 49–54, 64–5, 75, 87, 107, *see also* reported speech
spirits 8, 19, 58–60, 74–5, 110, *see also* shamans, sorcery, supernatural experience
Stallybrass, O. 20
Standard Estonian 102
Stenzel, Kristine 13, 19, 32, 54, 80, 84, 86, 93
Storch, Anne 7, 38, 40, 45, 48, 62–3, 69, 106
subordinate clause, *see* dependent clause
Sun, Jackson T.-S. 14, 16, 22–3, 35, 63, 72
supranatural experience 57, 77, 110, *see also* shamans, sorcery, spirits
surprise 16–17, 28–37, 41, 57, 109, 112, *see also* mirativity
Swanson, Tod D. 6

Tabo Tibetan 35
Tacanan languages 89, 95
Tagalog 93
Taku 35
Tariana 11–13, 18, 25–7, 33, 53, 82–4, 87–94, 97, 101, 103, 108–13
    access to information through evidentials 22–3
    awareness of evidentials 57–60
    changes in evidentials 60–1
    evidentials and tense 76, 86
    scope of evidentials 42
    shared knowledge through evidentials 74–80
    time reference of evidentials 53–4
Tarma Quechua 17, 42, 89
Tatar 24, 29, 60, 85, 89
Tatevosov, S. G. 100
Tatuyo 13, 37, 84, 89, 93
technology and the use of evidentials 8, 60–1
Telban, Borut 7

Telles, Stella   13, 71
Tena Kichwa   24
tense, *see* past tense, present tense
Thiesen, Wesley   57, 92
thirdhand evidential   13, 27, 32, 65, 71, 87
Thurgood, Graham   100
Tiang   41
Tibetan   14, 36, 88, *see also* Lhasa Tibetan
Tibetan languages   88
Tibetic languages   14
Tibeto-Burman languages   15, 20, 23, 35–6, 44, 49–51, 55, 63, 81, 88, 96, 100
Timberlake, Alan   20
time reference of evidentials   39, 53–5, 110
Tipton, Ruth A.   73
Tojolab'al   7
Tournadre, Nicolas   16, 88
Travis, Catherine   6, 30–1, 46–7
Trio   60, 98, 109
truth   4, 18, 24
Tsafiki   31–2, 36–7, 52
Tsakhur   30
Tsou   45–8, 93, 96, 105
Tucano   33, 42, 53, 59, 77, 83, 86–90, 93, 108
Tundra Nenets   48, 81, *see also* Nenets
Tungusic languages   21
Tupí-Guaraní languages   8, 13, 101
Turkic languages   23–4, 27, 89, 93, 100, 109
Turkish   28, 54
Tuyuca   11, 86, 101

Ugric languages   30
uncertainty   7, 18, 24–8, 36–7, 52, 88, 103, *see also* epistemic modality, certainty
unwitnessed evidential   30, 42, 60, 94, 100, 112, *see also* non-eyewitness evidential, non-firsthand evidential
Uralic languages   85
Urarina   97
Utas, Bo   5
Uto-Aztecan languages   35, 69

Valentine, J. Randolph   82, 92
Valenzuela, Pilar M.   27–8, 31, 42, 45, 55, 60, 90, 92, 96
Vallauri, E. L.   101
van der Auwera, J.   18
van der Voort, Hein   52

Vanrell, Maria del Mar   3
Vaupés River Basin linguistic area   10–11, 13, 32–3, 53–4, 61, 78, 83–4
verbs of cognition   83
verbs of perception   7, 83
verbs of speech   51
visual evidential   4, 10–14, 18, 22–7, 31–37, 48, 57–8, 61–3, 70–1, 74–8, 81–3, 86–92, 98, 101–110, *see also* direct evidential, firsthand evidential
volitional predicate   15, 30

Wa'ikhana, *see* Piratapuya
Wakashan languages   31, 85
Wälchli, Bernard   101–2
Wanano   32, 80
Wangdi, Pema   62, 96
Wanka Quechua   22–4, 33, 44
Warlbiri   96
Washo   31
Watters, Stephen   35–6, 40, 112
Wayana   60
Weber, David J.   24, 57, 92
West Himalayish languages   81
Western Apache   33–4
Western Nilotic languages   90
Wetzels, W. Leo   13, 71
WhatsApp   26, 61
Whistler, Kenneth W.   100
Widmer, Manuel   20
Wiemer, Björn   18, 23–4, 42, 81, 101
Wilcox, Sherman   3
Wilkins, D. P.   96
Willett, Thomas   5
Willis, Christina M.   81
Wiltschko, Martina   103
Wintu   59, 82, 109
Wissel Lakes languages   83
witnessed evidrntial   27, 33, 42–4, 57, 60, 77, 102, *see also* eyewitness evidential, firsthand evidential
Witotoan languages   81
Wojtylak, Katarzyna I.   57, 81, 92–3
Wola   73
Wood, Michael   60
Wrona, J.   101

!Xun   107, 109

Yang, Gloria Fan-pei 47, 105
Yang, Wenjiang 56–7
Yap, Foong-Ha 101
Yongning Na (Mosuo) 50–1, 63–5, 68, 110
Yukaghir 85
Yurakaré 81

Zeisler, Bettina 88
Zhang, Sihong 49–50, 88
Ziegeler, Deborah 82, 112
Zúñiga, Fernando 28

www.ingramcontent.com/pod-product-compliance
Lightning Source LLC
Chambersburg PA
CBHW071402290426
44108CB00014B/1660